GETTING STARTED WITH
WITH
Coding

2nd Edition
Camille McCue, PhD

WILEY

Getting Started with Coding, 2nd Edition

Published by
John Wiley & Sons, Inc.
111 River Street
Hoboken, NJ 07030-5774
www.wiley.com

For general information on our other products and services, please contact our Customer Care Department within the U.S. at 877-762-2974, outside the U.S. at 317-572-3993, or fax 317-572-4002. For technical support, please visit www.wiley.com/techsupport.

Wiley publishes in a variety of print and electronic formats and by print-on-demand. Some material included with standard print versions of this book may not be included in e-books or in print-on-demand. If this book refers to media such as a CD or DVD that is not included in the version you purchased, you may download this material at http://booksupport.wiley.com. For more information about Wiley products, visit www.wiley.com.

Library of Congress Control Number: 2019948336

ISBN 978-1-119-64162-9 (pbk); 978-1-119-64164-3 (epdf); 978-1-119-64163-6 (epub)

This book was produced using the Myriad Pro typeface for the body text and callouts, and Bangers for the chapter titles and subheads.

Manufactured in the United States of America

V10013910_091419

Contents

Project 3: Freeze the Pops   48

Project 4: Jellyfish Jumble 64

Project 5: Card War 83

INTRODUCTION

SO YOU WANT TO GET STARTED WITH CODING!
Writing computer programs, or *coding*, is a skill that
will take you from a user of technology to a maker
of technology. Coding is a skill that is fun, creative,
and productive. By discovering the language of the
computer, you become capable of inventing toys, games,
and apps that you can share with, well . . . everyone!

ABOUT THIS BOOK

You can use many computer languages to get
started with coding. What you find in this book is an
introduction to the big ideas and practices of coding,
using two coding languages: Scratch and JavaScript
block format, via MakeCode. You can learn more about
both languages in the next section, "What's New in the
Second Edition." The skills you build by coding projects
in this book can be used in every other programming
language.

Getting Started with Coding, 2nd Edition is put together
as a series of projects and related big ideas in coding.
Each project is presented as steps for constructing both
graphic design and code, start to finish. The big ideas
connect a project with the skills you'll perform over
and over again when coding. Best of all, projects can
be customized to bring to life the craziest ideas your
imagination can concoct!

Here's what you need to do the projects in this book:

> » A computer with a relatively modern version of a web
> browser (Safari, Chrome, or Firefox), or a tablet running
> Mobile Safari or Mobile Chrome. (Note that Internet
> Explorer is not supported.)

» An Internet connection.

» (Optional) A USB port on your computer and a micro:bit kit for transferring the electronics programs in this book to a physical board. A complete micro:bit kit retails for less than $20.

As you work through each project, keep in mind the following writing conventions:

» Code and web addresses are in monofont. If you're reading this as an ebook, you can click web addresses, like www.dummies.com, to visit that website.

» The highlighted text draws your attention to the figures.

» For each project, I give you step-by-step instructions. Instructions read "Drag an X into the Y" or "Click the X category and then click Y." Or I may simply tell you to click a link or a tab. Follow the instructions in order.

» Optional enhancements are given in each project so that you can customize your work to showcase your own creative ideas!

» Finally, every project wraps up with a last look at the project's big ideas in coding. The big ideas consist of concepts that lay the foundation for your future work in computer science.

That's all there is to it!

WHAT'S NEW IN THE SECOND EDITION

This second edition reflects recent trends in programming instruction. Specifically, this book uses programming languages that start you down the path of learning basic coding skills you can apply over and over as you learn more.

This edition of the book covers:

» **Scratch:** This learning language developed at MIT is so popular that it is arguably "the" starter programming language. As such, this book features several projects in the most recent version of Scratch — Scratch 3.0. (But for those of you who may be running an older, offline version of Scratch, you'll still be able to do most projects.) Scratch is a block-based language that lets new coders comfortably step into the world of computer programming. And it's fun!

» **JavaScript:** JavaScript is used in everything from apps to websites to electronics. Kids can begin learning in block-based mode of JavaScript, and then transition to text-based mode as they build skills and confidence in coding. In this book, JavaScript projects are presented through MakeCode, a platform for coding instructions that can operate a small electronics board called a micro:bit.

Best of all, the tools in this edition are free, available online, and easy-to-use.

ABOUT YOU

Everyone has to start somewhere, right? I had to start writing this book by assuming that you can do this stuff:

» Type on a computer and use a mouse (if you're working on a computer) or use a touch screen tablet (if you're working on a tablet). Your experience can be on Windows or Mac — or Android or iOS. Because Scratch and MakeCode run in a web browser, the instructions in this book are platform-independent. Figures show the programs as they would appear in Chrome on a Mac.

» Read or read with the help of someone who reads, as well as follow directions with help from the text and the figures.

» Do some basic math operations such as adding or comparing numbers. I introduce algebraic variables in this book, but you don't need to have any prior knowledge of variables.

Lastly, if you struggle with spelling and punctuation, you may need to spend extra time troubleshooting your code for misspellings. Block–based programming greatly reduces these types of errors, or bugs, and programming languages can give you clues about which commands they don't understand. But you will need to pay extra attention to the details, making certain that commands are written exactly as you intend.

ABOUT THE ICONS

As you read through the projects in this book, you'll see a few icons. The icons point out different things:

WARNING

Watch out! This icon marks important information that you can use to avoid common pitfalls when coding.

REMEMBER

The Remember icon marks concepts you've encountered before and should keep in mind while coding.

TIP

The Tip icon marks advice and shortcuts to make your work easier. You may see some tips several times in the book

TECHNICAL STUFF

The Technical Stuff icon give hardware help and tells you more about the nuts and bolts of technical details.

FUN WITH CODE

The Fun with Code icon describes how the coding you're doing relates to the bigger picture of computer programming.

FUN WITH MATH

The Fun with Math icon describes the everyday math you use while coding computer programs. Finally, you see how that stuff is really used!

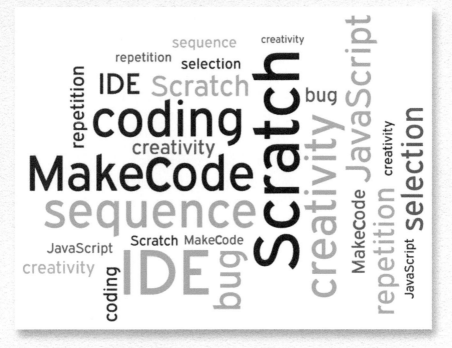

IT USED TO BE ENOUGH TO READ, WRITE, AND DO MATH. These three skills were the tools we needed to communicate with other human beings. But now, the world is full of smart beings that aren't human — they're computers. Computers don't fully think for themselves *yet*, but they do "talk" with each other and with people through *computer programming languages.* Communicating with technology — speaking the language of computers — takes a new skill called coding (also called programming). This chapter gets you started with the basics you'll need to start coding fast!

CODING QUICKSTART

Coding means writing instructions for a computer. The computer then uses the instructions to do a task.

A computer programming language has *commands* (vocabulary) and *syntax* (grammar rules and punctuation) for communicating with a computer. As you write code, you put together the commands, using the correct syntax, in a logical way. The *logic* of your code is the order of the commands and the sequence of what happens due to various conditions. Put together, the instructions that you write and that the computer reads are called the *computer program*, or just the *code*.

A HELLO WORLD! EXAMPLE

The first program new coders often write prints the words *Hello World!* on the computer screen. Here's the code in Scratch and its *output* (what it shows onscreen).

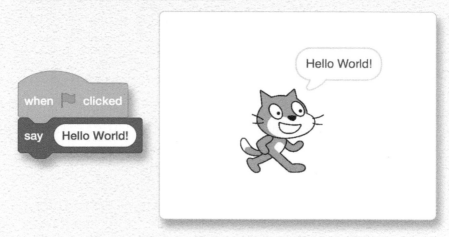

Now here's the same code in JavaScript blocks built in MakeCode and the output on the micro:bit electronics board. Because the micro:bit can scroll only one letter at a time, the figure displays just the letter *H* at the beginning of the *Hello World!* message.

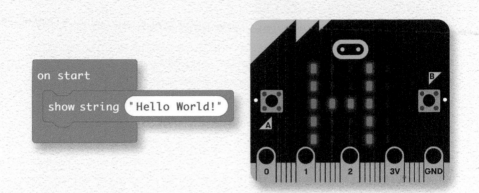

```
on start
    show string "Hello World!"
```

You'll be making little programs like this, and bigger programs too, in no time!

WHAT'S AN ALGORITHM?

A computer program has lots of parts, such as asking the user a question, doing something with that information, and then telling the user some response. Planning a computer program is a bit like telling a story or running a play in football. You have to put together and *execute* (run) the program in a certain order.

In each part of a program, you write small chunks of code to do different things. A chunk of code that does a task is called an *algorithm*. For example, in a paddle ball game, one algorithm you might use is bouncing the ball. If the ball and paddle touch, the player scores a point and the ball changes direction.

What algorithms do you see in games you play on your phone? One algorithm in a Yahtzee game is rolling the dice. An algorithm in a Space Invaders game is flying a spaceship across the sky. You also see algorithms in life, such as a pattern for vacuuming a room or a routine for driving to school. Look for algorithms in the apps you use and in your daily life.

SEQUENCE, SELECTION, AND REPETITION

The algorithms you write connect with each other to build your entire program. As coders, we have three fancy terms to describe how we build our algorithms and how they connect with each other: sequence, selection, and repetition. Here's what each means:

» **Sequence:** The order you run commands (or algorithms). Steps are executed one after another, in order. For example, when making pancakes, I run my algorithm for making batter before I run my algorithm for cooking the batter!

» **Selection:** Choose a path. For example, if you decide to go to a movie, you might then choose between an action movie and a comedy. That decision then directs you to new sequences: If you pick an action movie, you might then select among *Avengers, Pokémon,* and *Shazam!* You write selection code using *conditional* commands: if [this happens] then [do that]. Conditionals let you make as many paths as you need for your program.

» **Repetition:** Do something over and over. A *loop* tells the computer to run the same commands lots of times, without having to rewrite the commands. You already know how loops work: In a song, the drumbeat is looped to make the rhythm from the first note of the song to the last.

All computer programs have sequence, selection, and repetition. Check back here to refresh your memory of how each is used when coding a program.

FLOWCHARTING

As you plan your programs, you can make a special drawing — called a flowchart — to show your plan. A *flowchart* is like a little map with special boxes and arrows that show the smaller parts of the whole plan. You can plan almost anything with a flowchart — a travel schedule, a recipe, a basketball play, or an app you're making. This table shows some flowchart symbols and what each symbol means.

SYMBOLS USED IN FLOWCHARTS

Symbol	Name	What It Means
	Arrow	Shows the sequence of the program
	Terminal	Starts or ends the program
	Process	Does a task, such as a math problem
	Decision	Selects yes or no to follow a new path
	Input/output	Takes in information or tells the user something

In this book, you plan each program with a simple flowchart. Here's a flowchart for a program to decide on an afterschool activity. Planning a computer program with a flowchart helps you think about the big picture first. You can get your thinking straight and leave the details of writing code for later!

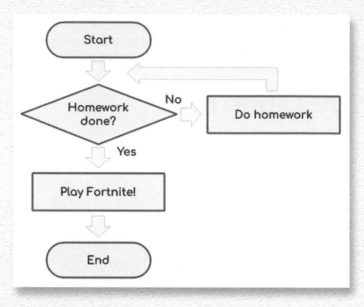

PICKING A LANGUAGE

As a coder, you pick a coding language depending on what you want to build. Some languages are good for building programs you run in a web browser, others are good for building phone apps, and still others are best for writing code to control electronic circuits.

In this book, you use Scratch, a kids programming language, to make an animation, a toy puzzle, and a game for a computer or tablet. You also use JavaScript, a real programming language, to code electronic gadgets. In JavaScript, you make for the micro:bit board a thermometer and a game of card war. In both Scratch and JavaScript, you can work in *block mode*, snapping together code by using tile (puzzle) pieces to build your programs.

USING A DASHBOARD (IDE)

No matter what language you choose, you need a way to write and test your code in that language — a *coding dashboard*. Real coders use a special name for the dashboard: *integrated development environment*, or *IDE*. A coding IDE, or dashboard, is an all-in-one place where you do all the things needed to create your code and make it ready for end users. *End users* are the people who will use your programs.

The dashboards you will use are web-based, meaning you go to a website and do your work online. Scratch has its own dashboard, and JavaScript can be written in many different IDEs — in this book, you use the MakeCode dashboard to write code in block-based JavaScript. In the dashboard, you do these things:

» **Write code.** You write code by dragging code tiles (individual blocks) to a workspace and snapping them together to build larger code blocks.

» **Create the screen layout.** Put together *assets* — such as sounds and graphics — to display onscreen in your program.

» **Compile your code.** *Compiling* means translating your code from a human-friendly form to one that the computer understands. Scratch and MakeCode do this for you automatically.

» **Debug.** You debug your code by editing it to fix any errors, or *bugs*. Bugs cause your program to not work.

» **Test.** You try out your code in a display window or simulator.

The following sections help you set up and understand the Scratch and MakeCode dashboards.

SETTING UP YOUR ACCOUNT IN SCRATCH

Scratch is free, but you need to set up an account before you can start coding. Just follow these steps:

1 **In any web browser, navigate to https://scratch.mit.edu.**

2 **On the Scratch home page, select Join Scratch.**

3 **In the Scratch dialog box, type a Scratch username and a password. Then click the Next button.**

4 **Type your birthdate, gender, and country. Then click Next.**

5 **Type the email of your parent or guardian. Then click Next.**

A screen appears letting you know that you are signed up to use Scratch and that a confirmation email has been sent to your parent or guardian.

6 **Your parent or guardian must open the email and confirm that you're permitted to share your work publicly on Scratch.**

If the adult doesn't confirm, you can still work in Scratch, but you won't be able to share your programs.

7 **Click OK on the final screen to complete the sign-up.**

After your Scratch account is set up, you can log in to your account at any time by clicking the Sign In button in the upper right of the Scratch home page and typing your username and password.

GETTING AROUND IN SCRATCH

After you set up your Scratch account, you are taken to the Scratch home page. Here are some of the things you'll see, and some of the actions you can perform.

Select Create in the menu bar on the Scratch home page to open the Scratch dashboard. In the Scratch dashboard, you see a new, blank project. This is the same screen you see if you choose File ⇨ New when working in Scratch.

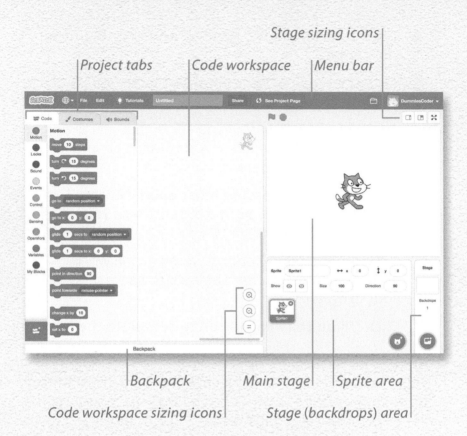

Stage sizing icons

Project tabs | Code workspace | Menu bar

Backpack | Main stage | Sprite area

Code workspace sizing icons | Stage (backdrops) area

The *menu bar* at the top of the Scratch dashboard features just a few choices. These are the most important:

» **File ⇨ New:** Create a new project.

» **Edit:** Turn Turbo mode on or off. When on, this mode runs the program superfast.

» **Project name field:** Name your project.

» **Share button:** Share your project.

» **See Project Page button:** Go to the project page for your current project, where you can tell users how to use your program. On the project page, click the See Inside button to get back to the Scratch dashboard.

» **My Stuff folder icon:** Open projects you've created.

The *tabs* on the left side of the Scratch dashboard change depending on whether you're creating code for a *sprite* (an object in Scratch) or for the *main stage* (the backdrop where your sprites live):

» **Code tab:** Command categories and their blocks

» **Costumes tab:** Sprite costumes and the costume editor

» **Backdrops tab:** Backdrops for the stage and the backdrop editor

» **Sounds tab:** Sounds and the sound editor

The *workspace* is the place where you drag command blocks and then assemble those command blocks together to make larger *code blocks.* Click the *sizing icons* to zoom in or zoom out as you build code.

The *backpack* area at the bottom of the Scratch dashboard is a place where you can save, store, and reuse project items, sharing them among projects. Just drag a code block, sprite, costume, or sound into the backpack and it will be available in all projects! Drag an item from the backpack and into a project's workspace to use it. Delete an item in the backpack by Ctrl-clicking (Mac) or right-clicking (Windows) the item.

The *main stage* is the large window that shows you what your user sees. Here, you can see the sprites and the backdrop. Click a *stage sizing icon* to resize your view of the stage. Above the stage are the *green flag* and *stop* icons; use these to start or stop most projects you create.

The *sprite area* shows the sprites (objects) in your project. Each time you start a new project, the Scratch Cat sprite is added by default (something the computer does automatically) and named Sprite1. You can find out more information about Sprite1 in the Sprite area, just below the main stage. The Sprite area tells you the sprite's position on the main stage (the x and y values), whether the sprite is showing or hiding (the eyeball icons), its size, and its direction. To delete a sprite, click the X in the corner of the sprite icon. To add a new sprite, click the *choose a sprite* icon (which looks like a kitty head with a plus sign).

The small *stage*, or *backdrops* area, is located in the lower-right corner of the Scratch dashboard. Here, an icon shows the current backdrop. Clicking this icon makes the stage active, which means you can write code for the stage, change which backdrop shows in the background, and add sounds to the background.

WARNING

To write code for a sprite or the stage, you first click its icon to select it, or make it active. The active icon has a blue outline. Only one sprite or the stage can be active at a time, so pay attention to which of these is currently selected.

USING THE CODE TAB IN SCRATCH

The Scratch dashboard in the previous figure is shown with the Code tab selected. This tab has all the commands you can use in your programs. You use this tab for both sprites and the stage. It is organized by command categories, as follows:

» **Motion (blue):** Commands to tell sprites (objects) how and where to move. (The stage does not have motion commands.)

» **Looks (purple):** Commands to change the costumes of sprites and change which backdrop is on the stage background.

» **Sound (pink):** Commands to play music and sound effects.

» **Events (yellow):** Commands to start and end code execution.

» **Control (light orange):** Commands to select code or repeat code for execution. (See the "Sequence, selection, and repetition" section for details.)

» **Sensing (light blue):** Commands to sense color, sound, position, and user input.

» **Operators (green):** Commands for math and logic operations.

» **Variables (dark orange):** Commands to create and change variables.

» **My Blocks (red):** New commands you define for your project.

» **Add extension (wavy lines):** Access to additional commands you can add in Scratch 3.0, such as text-to-speech and language translation.

To write code for a sprite or the stage, click a command category. Then drag one block (command) from the category and drop it into the workspace. Add the next command by dragging a new block below the previous one and then snapping it (bringing it close) to build a code block. Remove a command by clicking it and dragging it back to the command categories (anywhere). To *execute*, or run, the code block, click the block. The code block will light up with a bright yellow outline, and the commands in that block will execute.

Scratch automatically saves your projects in the cloud, but you can also save at any time by choosing File ⇨ Save Now from the menu bar.

GETTING AROUND IN MAKECODE

MakeCode doesn't require you to create an account. Access the MakeCode site shown here at https:// makecode.microbit.org. This is your page for creating a new project, opening projects you've made, and seeing sample projects and tutorials for lots of other projects you can program for the micro:bit. You can get back to this page at any time by clicking the Home button at the top of the page.

When you create a new project in MakeCode, you see the MakeCode dashboard (IDE) shown here.

Simulator | Menu bar | Code toolbox | Workspace

Slo-mo icon

Download button | Save icon

Play/stop icon | Project name

Undo/redo icons

Zoom icons

The *menu bar* at the top of the MakeCode dashboard features just a few choices. These are the most important:

» **Home button:** Return to the MakeCode home page.

» **Share button:** Share your project.

» **Blocks/JavaScript toggle:** Choose to code in blocks or JavaScript text mode.

The micro:bit *simulator,* which is the window on the left, shows what your user sees. It acts the way a micro:bit does, except it's digital (not a real, physical electronics board). Here, you can see and run your program to get everything working before you transfer your program to the micro:bit. The simulator icons you can click are

» **Play:** Run your program. (This icon looks like an arrowhead.)

» **Stop:** Stop program execution.

» **Restart:** Reset the program to the start.

» **Slo-mo:** Slow the rate of program execution, a helpful tool when debugging. (This icon looks like a snail.)

» **Audio:** Mute or unmute sound.

» **Full screen:** Make your micro:bit simulator appear in a large format on its own screen.

The *workspace* is the place where you drag command blocks and put commands together to build your *program*. Click the *zoom in* or *zoom out* icon in the bottom-right corner to adjust your view. If needed, you can click the *undo* or *redo* icon in the bottom-right corner to edit your code.

The *debug console* is a window that appears below the simulator if you have an error in your code. This console gives you clues about mistakes in your program and where to look to fix them.

TIP

In this book, you write JavaScript code in block mode using command blocks (also known as tiles). But you can also write in text-based mode by clicking the JavaScript button in the menu bar of the MakeCode dashboard. To switch back to blocks mode, click the Blocks button.

USING THE CODE TOOLBOX IN MAKECODE

MakeCode's *code toolbox* provides coding commands for you to build your micro:bit programs. Here are the categories of commands:

» **Basic:** Commands to show images or text by using the LEDs, as well as the on start and forever commands.

» **Input:** Commands to read user input, such as a button click, a shake of the micro:bit board, or an electrical signal from one of the pins.

» **Music:** Commands for playing music. Sound can play in the simulator, but the micro:bit does not have a built-in speaker, so you need to hook up headphones or a speaker to make the micro:bit produce sound.

» **Led:** Commands for making the LEDs light up individually.

» **Radio:** Commands for having micro:bits talk to each other by using a radio frequency.

» **Loops:** Commands for doing repeats.

» **Logic:** Commands for making decisions (conditionals, comparisons, and Booleans).

» **Variables:** Commands to make and change the value of a variable.

» **Math:** Commands for doing math.

To write code, select a command category and then drag and drop one block (command tile) into the workspace. Add the next command by dragging it below the previous one and then bringing it close to snap the tiles together, building your program. Delete a command by clicking it and dragging it back to the code toolbox. (Or in text-mode, select the command you want to get rid of and then click the Delete key on your keyboard.) To *execute,* or run, the program on the simulator, click the *play* icon.

To *save* your program, type the name of your program in the Untitled field at the bottom of the MakeCode dashboard and then click the *save* icon.

MakeCode for micro:bit offers Advanced commands, with lots of other command categories. These commands let you build even more complex programs. If you want to challenge yourself, check them out!

FIXING ERRORS

Your code probably won't be perfect the first time you write it. Whether you're just starting out coding or you've been programming for a while, you — like everyone else — will make mistakes when writing code. As a coder, you will spend a lot of time fixing those mistakes, or *bugs,* in your programs. (They're called *bugs* because one of the "mistakes" in the early days of computing was an actual bug in the computer's electronic circuitry!)

You will need to find your errors and fix them before your programs can run. Fixing mistakes in your code is called *debugging.* Here are the two types of bugs you will need to remove:

» **Syntax errors:** When the form of the code is wrong — you spelled something wrong or messed up your punctuation — you get a *syntax error.* Block coding makes it hard to make syntax errors because there's almost no typing and the blocks fit together in specific ways. But if a syntax error does happen, you must fix this mistake or else the program won't run.

» **Logic errors:** When the behavior of the code is wrong, you get a *logic error*. For example, if the game score goes down each time a hero defeats an enemy, you may have coded a score variable to decrease, not increase. The code runs because the syntax is correct, but the program doesn't do what you want it to do. At that point, you need to figure out what is going wrong, and then find the part of your code that controls the behavior that is not working correctly.

Testing your program means running it to see if it works the way you want it to. The following sections give you some strategies for debugging your code in Scratch and in MakeCode.

DEBUGGING IN SCRATCH

Scratch helps stop you from making syntax errors because you don't type the commands. Instead, you drag command blocks into the code workspace. You don't have to worry about misspelling a command or forgetting to add a semicolon because Scratch prevents you from making these types of errors. Instead of typing a premade element such as a variable name, for example, you select it from a drop-down list.

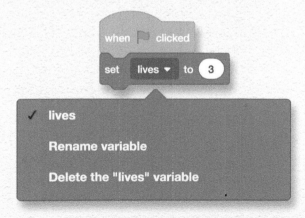

When coding in Scratch, you're likely to make mistakes in the logic of your program. Because you see these mistakes when you run your program, they are called *runtime errors.* To fix this type of error, you try to find the exact place where something is going wrong in the execution of your program. Then you change the code to correct your error (or errors).

Here are some ways to locate and fix runtime errors in Scratch:

» **Focus on one sprite at a time.** If a sprite is working the way you want, move on to the next sprite and check its operation. (In many projects, you also write code for the stage, and you can use this method to check the stage as well.)

» **When you find a sprite with a runtime error, run the program a few times to see what the sprite is doing.** Try to figure out exactly what is going wrong and when that behavior occurs.

» **Look carefully at the code for the sprite with the runtime error.** Step through the code one command at a time. Separate some of the code (remove it temporarily by dragging it to the side, away from the event command). Then add sections of your code back in, one command at a time, and test the operation of the sprite after each addition. You should be able to identify where the error is occurring. At this point, fixing the error is usually easy.

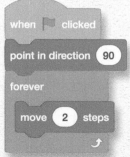

Here's an example of a logic, or runtime, error in Scratch. I want my butterfly to fly toward the left of the screen, but it's flying toward the right. I think to myself, "Hmmm, my butterfly is flying, and he's flying at the speed I want. But he's going the wrong way. Maybe I set my direction wrong."

So I look at the part of my code that has to do with direction. I see that I have set the direction to positive 90, pointing the butterfly to the right. I should have set the direction to negative 90 (by typing –90), pointing the butterfly to the left. So I type the correct value and test my code to make sure it is fixed.

DEBUGGING IN MAKECODE

The block mode of MakeCode is like Scratch — it helps keep you from making syntax errors. Because you use premade blocks (also called command tiles), you can't type misspellings or forget to include punctuation.

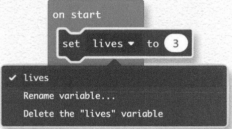

When coding in MakeCode using blocks, any errors will probably happen at runtime. If you run a MakeCode program in the micro:bit simulator and get an error, an Explorer window appears just below the micro:bit simulator. The MakeCode Explorer window displays the number of errors in the program.

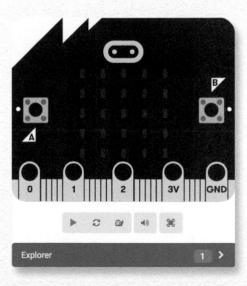

You can click the Explorer window to expand it and view more information about the execution of your program and the errors. But be aware that it's a bit hard for new coders to read and understand the Explorer window!

Your best bet for fixing runtime errors in MakeCode is to run the program a few times and trace the code as it runs, step-by-step. Try to pinpoint the exact moment when an error takes place, and then go to that part of the code and look closely at it. Change the code to fix your error (or errors).

TIP

Click the slo-mo icon in the simulator to slow the program speed, making it easier to trace the action.

Remember, half of coding is writing the code — and the other half is debugging it!

GETTING HELP

This book covers just a few key commands in Scratch and MakeCode. For more help, the Scratch home page has a Search field in the menu bar, where you can type a search term to get information on that topic. In MakeCode, go to https://makecode.microbit.org/reference to look up how to use a command. Also, when working in the MakeCode dashboard, hover your cursor over any command tile to see a tip with information on the command.

Additionally, both Scratch and MakeCode offer tutorials and project samples at https://scratch.mit.edu/ideas and https://microbit.org/ideas. Every example that you view, play with, and code yourself is a learning opportunity!

PROJECT 2 JUNGLE CHAT

DO YOU LIKE ANIMALS IN THE JUNGLE? If so, you'll love the project in this chapter! You code a fun scene with characters that make animal sounds and speak your name. This coding project introduces you to some big ideas in coding, including event-driven programming and sequence — when you click an animal (the event), you start the execution of code that runs one command after another (the sequence). The scene also helps you learn about inputs and outputs (also called I/O), joining strings of text, text-to-speech, parallel processing, and user interfaces.

Let's get coding!

BRAINSTORM

In this project, you work in Scratch to create your own nature scene for viewing on a computer or tablet. Your scene uses assets from the Scratch libraries. *Assets* are sprites, backgrounds, and sounds you use to build what the user sees and hears. You can create a realistic scene such as jungle animals in the jungle. Or you can create something wacky by mixing animals and objects together in weird ways, such as putting a giraffe and a car in the snow!

FLOWCHART

Plan your Jungle Chat program by drawing a flowchart to show how the program will run. The flowchart doesn't need to have every step; include just the main parts.

I know that I want to make a monkey who lives in the jungle and talks! To do this, I need to add a Monkey sprite. Then I will write code so that the monkey does something when a user clicks him.

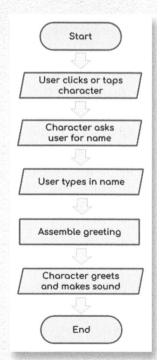

In my flowchart, I want the Monkey click event to run a sequence of commands. In this sequence, the Monkey will ask for the user's name and then store what the user types. Next, the Monkey will make a greeting. The greeting will be shown and spoken. Last, the Monkey will make a "chee-chee" sound. Here's my flowchart for the program I will write — your flowchart may look similar.

START A NEW PROJECT

Begin creating your Jungle Chat program by starting a new project:

1 **Open Scratch at** https://scratch.mit.edu.

2 **On the Scratch home page, select Create.**

Or if you're already working in Scratch, choose File ⇨ New Project from the menu bar. A new project opens.

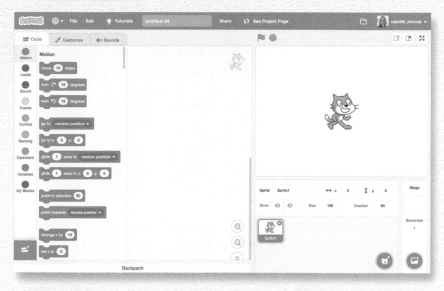

3 **Name your program by typing a name in the project name field at the top of the Scratch dashboard.**

I named my program Jungle Chat.

4 **Cut (delete) Scratch Cat from the project by clicking or tapping the X in the Scratch Cat icon.**

You can find the icon in the sprite area in the lower-right corner of the Scratch dashboard.

ADD A BACKDROP

The *backdrop* is the background color or image that fills the screen of your animated toy. To add a backdrop:

1 **At the stage, click the choose a backdrop icon.**

(Be sure to click the icon, not hover your cursor over it. Hovering makes a pop-up menu appear where you can create your backdrop other ways.) The backdrop library appears on the Choose a Backdrop screen. The library is organized by theme and has categories such as Music and Sports.

REMEMBER

To go back to the previous view of backdrops, click or tap Back, in the upper-left corner.

2 **Click or tap the Outdoors button to narrow your backdrop choices to an outdoors theme.**

The library now displays only backdrops showing the outdoors.

TIP

Use the search box in the backdrop library to find the name of a backdrop theme, such as Desert. If the backdrop exists, it will appear.

3 **From the list of backdrops, click or tap the backdrop you want.**

Your backdrop appears on the stage. I chose the Jungle backdrop for my program.

ADD ANIMAL SPRITES

Programming languages have ways to make objects. In Scratch, an *object* is a thing that appears on the computer screen — a car, bird, paintball, and so on. Scratch calls these objects sprites. A *sprite* is an object that "lives" in a backdrop.

You can add an animal sprite to your scene by following these steps:

1 **In the sprite area of the Scratch interface, click the choose a sprite icon.**

(Be sure to click the icon, not hover your cursor over it. Hovering makes a pop-up menu appear.) The sprite library appears on the Choose a Sprite screen. The library shows categories, such as Animals and Food.

2 Click or tap the Animals button to narrow your sprite choices to an animal theme.

The library now displays only animal sprites.

To go back to the previous view of the sprites, click or tap Back.

REMEMBER

3 In the list of animal sprites, click or tap the sprite you want.

Your sprite appears on the stage. I picked the Monkey sprite!

4 Click the sprite (not the icon) on the main stage and drag it where you want.

5 If you want to, resize your animal by typing a new number in the Size field above the sprite.

The default (starting) size of a sprite is 100. I left my monkey at size 100.

6 Repeat Steps 1–5 to add and size more animals for your scene. I added two more animals, a snake at size 60 and a toucan at size 80.

Each new sprite appears on the stage. An icon for each sprite also appears in the sprite area of the Scratch dashboard. The figure shows all three animal sprites, sized and on the Jungle backdrop.

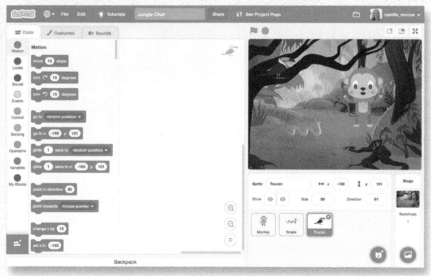

When resizing, select the icon of the sprite you want before typing a number in its size field.

REMEMBER

Your user interface is now complete! A *user interface* is what the user sees when using your program. The Jungle Chat user interface has a stage with a backdrop and three animal sprites.

REMEMBER

If you decide you don't want a sprite, cut it by clicking or tapping the X in its icon.

ADD TEXT-TO-SPEECH COMMANDS

When your jungle animals greet, the user will hear and see the words. Add text-to-speech commands to your Scratch dashboard as follows:

1 **Click or tap the add extension icon in the lower-left corner of the Scratch interface.**

2 **In the dialog box, click or tap the Text to Speech box.**

Text-to-speech commands are added to your commands.

Text to Speech
Make your projects talk.

Requires   Collaboration with

🛜   **Amazon Web Services**

CODE THE MONKEY TO RUN WHEN CLICKED

Next, you need to code an animal sprite to greet the user when the user clicks on it with a mouse or taps it on a touchpad. This action is an *event*. *Event-driven programming* is just a fancy way of saying that when an event occurs — such as a user clicking a mouse or tapping something on a mobile device — the computer program does something.

Simply follow these steps:

1 **Select an animal sprite.**

I chose the Monkey sprite. You can see that the Monkey sprite icon has a blue outline.

2 **On the Code tab of the Scratch interface, select the Events icon.**

The Events commands appear.

3 **Drag a** `when this sprite clicked` **event command to the code workspace.**

CODE THE MONKEY TO ASK THE USER'S NAME

Next, you need to code the sprite to ask the user to type his or her name. To do this, use the built-in ask command. You then store the name in the built-in answer variable. A *variable* is a place where you can store information that changes. (I talk more about variables later!) Next, you make the greeting by joining the *string literal* (the words that don't change) with the variable (the user's name). Finally, you display the greeting and speak the greeting.

Simply follow these steps:

1 **Keep coding the Monkey sprite. Select the Sensing icon to see the sensing commands. Drag an** ask **and** wait **command to the code workspace, and attach it to the previous command.**

2 **Leave the default question in the** ask **field (**What's your name?**), or type a new question.**

When the program runs, it shows a blank text field for the user to type a response. The program just waits for the user before going to the next command in the sequence. After she types her name and clicks the checkmark button next to the text entry field (or presses Enter or Return on the keyboard), her text will be stored in the answer variable.

TIP

Unlike most programming languages, including JavaScript, Scratch doesn't require quotes around a string literal such as What's your name?

MAKE AND GIVE THE GREETING

The next commands in your program sequence will make and give the greeting to the user. To do this, you will need to `join` the user's name with some other text. Then, you can use the `say` command to show the greeting in a speech bubble onscreen. And you can use the `text-to-speech` command to speak the greeting. Here's how:

1 **Keep coding on the Monkey sprite. Select the Looks icon. Drag a** `say` **command and attach it to the previous command.**

2 **Select the Operators icon. Drag a** `join` **command to the code workspace, and place it inside the field of the** `say` **command.**

3 **In the first field of the** `join` **command, type your greeting.**

I typed `Hello` in the field. Note that this text literal has a space after the word.

4 **Select the Sensing icon. Drag an** `answer` **variable inside the second field of the** `join` **command.**

The value of the answer variable — whatever name the user typed — is inserted into the greeting.

5 **Select the Text to Speech icon, drag a** `set  voice to` **command to the code workspace, and attach it to the previous command. Select a voice from the menu in the command.**

I chose the squeak voice (because my monkey has a squeaky voice).

6 Still working with the Text to Speech commands, drag a speak command to the code workspace, and attach it to the previous command.

7 Create the same join Hello answer greeting you made in Steps 2–4.

Or Ctrl-click (Mac) or right-click (Windows) the greeting and select Duplicate from the pop-up menu. Then place the greeting inside the empty field of the speak command.

REMEMBER

When you select a new sprite, you see only the code associated with that sprite. Don't panic — you haven't lost any code!

CODE THE MONKEY TO PLAY A SOUND

The Monkey sprite has two built-in sounds called Chee Chee and Chomp. Make him play the sound you want after he finishes his greeting.

1 Continue working on the Monkey sprite, and continue working at the Code tab.

2 Select the Sound icon. Drag the play sound until done command to the code workspace and attach it to the previous command.

3 Click or tap the
   down arrow on the
   play sound until
   done command and
   select the sound you
   want for the Monkey
   sprite.

   I chose the Chee
   Chee sound.

The code block for the
Monkey sprite is now
complete!

```
when this sprite clicked

ask    What's your name?    and wait

say    join    Hello      answer

       set voice to    squeak ▾

       speak    join    Hello    answer

play sound    Chee Chee ▾    until done
```

CODE THE SNAKE TO PLAY A SOUND YOU RECORD

You can make your other animals play sounds
when clicked. You can even record your
own sound! Record a hissing sound for the
Snake sprite, for example, by following these
directions:

1 In the sprite area, click the Snake sprite.
   Switch to the Sounds tab.

2 Hover your cursor over (or press down on)
   the choose a sound icon and click or tap the
   record icon.

3 At the Record Sound dialog box, click or tap
   the orange Record button and begin recording your
   sound.

   The sound loudness level and sound waveform are
   displayed as you record.

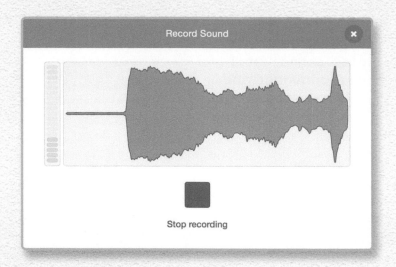

4 **When you have finished recording, click or tap the Stop Recording button.**

Your recorded sound is added to the Sounds tab for the Snake sprite. The default name of the sound is recording1. You can type a new name for the sound, such as hiss, in the Sound field.

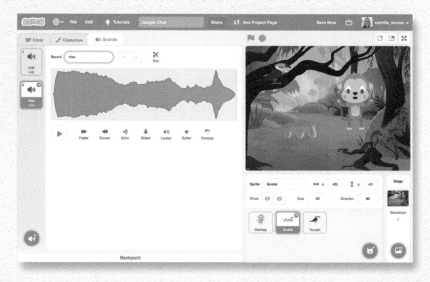

On a sprite, you can delete a sound by clicking the X on its icon.

TIP

5 **On the Code tab, select the Events icon.**

The Events commands appear.

6 **Drag a** when this sprite clicked **event command to the code workspace.**

7 **Select the Sound icon. Drag the** play sound until done **command to the code workspace and attach it to the previous command.**

8 **Click or tap the tab on the** play sound **command tile and select the sound you recorded for the Snake sprite.**

I chose the hiss sound.

The code block for the Snake sprite is now complete!

CODE THE TOUCAN TO PLAY A SOUND FROM THE SOUND LIBRARY

You've learned how to use a sound built into a sprite and how to record your own sound. Here, you choose a sound from the sound library. Add a bird sound to the Toucan sprite as follows:

1 **In the sprite area, click the Toucan sprite. Switch to the Sounds tab.**

2 **Click or tap the choose a sound icon.**

The sound library opens.

3 **At the sound library, click or tap a sound you want to add to your Toucan sprite.**

PROJECT 2 JUNGLE CHAT

I clicked the Animals category of the sound library and listened to the available sounds. Strangely, toucans sound a lot like jungle frogs, so I chose the Jungle Frogs sound. Your selected sound is added to the Sounds tab for the Toucan sprite.

4 On the Code tab, select the Events icon.

The Events commands appear.

5 Drag a when this sprite clicked event command to the code workspace.

6 Select the Sound icon. Drag the play sound until done command to the code workspace and attach it to the previous command.

7 Click or tap the down arrow on the play sound command tile and select the sound you chose for the Toucan sprite.

I chose the Jungle
Frogs sound.

The code block for
the Toucan sprite is
now complete!

FUN WITH
CODE

If you click the sprites quickly, one after another, each sprite begins running its commands while the other sprites are still executing their commands. The sounds they make overlap, making a chorus of jungle music! This behavior is an example of parallel processing.

ENHANCE YOUR SCENE

Consider enhancing your nature scene with new features:

» **New animals:** Add new animals, real or fantasy, for the user to play with.

» **New sounds:** Add new sounds from the sound library or sounds that you record, for your user to try out.

» **New sounds online:** Tons of music loops, vocals, and sound effects are available in sound libraries on the web. See Project 7 for additional information.

» **Single-event start:** Why bother clicking or tapping each sprite to run its code? Replace the when this sprite clicked event in each sprite with a when green flag clicked command. All the sprites will start running their code blocks with a single event (a click of the green flag)!

SAVE, TEST, AND DEBUG YOUR PROGRAM

As you work, Scratch automatically saves your program in the cloud, so you don't have to take any special actions to save your work. Test your program by clicking each animal to make sure it speaks or plays sounds as you planned. Fix any bugs so that the entire program works the way you want it to. (For help, see the section in Project 1 on debugging Scratch programs.)

SHARE YOUR PROGRAM WITH THE WORLD

After your program operates perfectly, it's time to share it! Set the status of your program to Share, and then add to your project page a description of your program and directions on how to run it. See Project 7 for details on sharing your programs.

BIG IDEAS IN THE PROJECT

Event-driven programming: In an *event-driven program,* events affect how the program runs. An event can be a user action such as a button click. Or an event can be triggered by a sensor, such as a thermometer reading a high or low temperature. Lastly, an event can be triggered when it gets information from another part of the program. In this project, events are user clicks of sprites.

Input and output (I/O): *Input* means something put into a program, for example, your name in a game app. *Output* means something that comes out of a program, for example, a message announcing that you got the high score! You will often see *input and output* written as *I/O*. In computer programs, inputs and outputs let you "talk" with your devices and let your devices "talk" with you! In this project, the user inputs a name and the program outputs a greeting.

Joining text (concatenating): *Joining* means connecting text pieces to build a phrase or sentence. You can join *literals* (text that doesn't change) and *string variables* (text that can change, such as a name) in any way you want. This process is also called *concatenating*. Jungle Chat joins the user's name with other text to make a greeting.

Parallel processing: This term means that the computer program runs different blocks of code at the same time (in parallel) so you can have more than one thing happening in your program at once. It's like using your left hand to pat your head and using your right hand to rub your tummy; your actions occur *concurrently* (at the same time). You can make the events in Jungle Chat run in parallel by replacing sprite clicks with a green flag event to start code running at the same time.

Program sequence: Computer code runs one command after another within a code block, in order. Each animal sprite in the project runs a sequence of code.

User interface (UI): The *user interface* is the way a person uses your program. It is usually a screen of pictures and text, with buttons or other items to click or tap to make the program do something. A user interface can also be a remote control, a code keypad, or an Alexa (which uses speech to interact). In this project, the UI was a scene with animal objects for the user to click.

PROJECT 3 FREEZE THE POPS

Image source: https://upload.wikimedia.org/wikipedia/commons/5/51/Freezies-in-freezer.jpg

WAITING FOR ICE POPS TO FREEZE FEELS LIKE FOREVER! Why waste time jiggling the pops to see if they're squishy or solid when you can code a gadget that lets you know your pops are ready? This project introduces you to coding for simple electronics so you can build and code a real Freeze the Pops thermometer! You'll work with a temperature sensor and selection — when the pops reach a freezing temperature, your gadget will alert you. Working on this gadget also helps you learn about coding simple math, making and using a variable, selection using conditionals, and optionally sending information from a sensor to your smartphone.

You can simulate the gadget on your computer, or you can make a real gadget if you have a micro:bit.

Let's get coding!

BRAINSTORM

In this project, you work in Scratch to make your own *Internet of Things (IoT)* monitor, which means you use a sensor to measure something and send the information somewhere else. Follow the directions for this project exactly to make a gadget for measuring the temperature of ice pops as they cool down in the freezer. Or make a different type of thermometer, one that measures something else. What about a thermometer for measuring when it's hot enough outside to go for a swim, or using your gadget for a science experiment? You can read the temperature of wherever the micro:bit is located and, optionally, send the value to your smartphone by using a *Bluetooth* connection (a wireless connection between devices). For instructions, see the online guide at www.dummies.com/gettingstartedwithcoding. You choose what project you want to build.

FLOWCHART

Plan your Freeze the Pops program by drawing a flowchart to show how the program will run. Your flowchart should have just the main parts; it doesn't need to have every step.

When I think about my program, I know that I want to make a gadget that checks the temperature of my freezer pops. To do this, I need to press a button to make the micro:bit display the temperature.

I will write code so that the button press makes the micro:bit thermometer read and display the temperature of the pops.

In my flowchart, I want the press Button A event to run a sequence of commands. In this sequence, the temperature sensor will be read in degrees Celsius. Then the Celsius number will be converted to Fahrenheit (F), and the program will display this number. Next, I want to code some selection. If the pops are more than 32 degrees F, I want the micro:bit to show WAIT. But if the pops are 32 degrees F or less, I want the micro:bit to show FREEZE. Here's my flowchart for the program I will write.

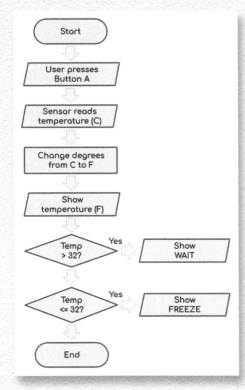

START A NEW PROJECT

Begin creating your Freeze the Pops control program by starting a new project:

1 **Open MakeCode for micro:bit at** https:// makecode.microbit.org.

2 **On the MakeCode home page, click the big purple New Project button.**

   Or if you're already working in MakeCode, choose Home from the menu bar and then click the New Project button. A new project opens.

3 **Drag the** on start **and** forever **commands into the command categories area to recycle them — you won't need them for now.**

4 **Name your project by typing a name in the Project Name field at the bottom of the MakeCode dashboard.**

Before you name your project, the field shows *Untitled*. I named my project Temperature, but you can name yours anything you want.

Temperature	💾

5 Click the Save icon (an old-school floppy disk) next to the Project Name field to save your project.

MAKE A VARIABLE

A *variable* is a storage container that holds a value that can change over time. Computer programs have different types of variables: numbers, strings (text, such as your name, like in Project 2), and Booleans (true or false). In this project, you want to measure the changing temperature as the freezer pops cool. Because the value changes, you will use a temperature variable in your code.

1 In the Variables category of commands, click the Make a Variable button.

2 In the New Variable Name dialog box, type a variable name for the temperature you will measure.

New variable name:

degreesF

Ok ✔	Cancel ✖

I used degreesF because we want to store the temperature measurement in degrees Fahrenheit, a common way to measure temperature.

3 Click OK.

The degreesF variable is added to the list of variables you can use in your MakeCode project.

FUN WITH MATH

Three ways to tell the temperature are Fahrenheit, Celsius, and Kelvin. Water freezes at 32 degrees Fahrenheit, 0 degrees Celsius, and 273 degrees Kelvin. The U.S. measures temperature in Fahrenheit, but most countries use Celsius. To convert from one scale to another, you use simple math (adding, subtracting, multiplying, and dividing).

CODE BUTTON A TO MEASURE AND SHOW THE TEMPERATURE

To build your code, you drag blocks into the MakeCode workspace. You will write an *event-driven* program to run when the Button A is pressed. (See Project 2 for help on event-driven programming.) The micro:bit measures temperature in degrees Celsius, but you will convert this to degrees Fahrenheit. Complete these steps:

1 **In the Input category of commands, drag an** `on button A pressed` **command to the workspace.**

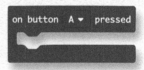

When the end user presses Button A, it will run the code block (which you create in the next steps).

2 **In the Variable category of commands, drag a** `set degreesF` **command to the workspace and drop it inside the** `on button A pressed` **command.**

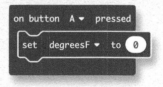

You can set the variable to any variable in your program by clicking the down arrow on the command tile at the variable name. The tile shows a default value of 0. You'll replace this number in the next step.

3 In the Math category of commands, drag a round **command to the workspace. Insert this command in the** set degreesF **command, replacing the** 0.

The round command will round any number that follows it. We don't want a bunch of icky decimals scrolling across our micro:bit screen!

4 **In the Math category of commands, drag a** 0 + 0 **command to the workspace. Insert this command in the** round **command, replacing the** 0. **Type the number** 32 **in the first field, replacing the first** 0.

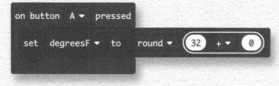

5 **In the Math category of commands, drag a** 0 x 0 **command to the workspace. Insert this command in the** 32 + 0 **command, replacing the** 0. **Type the number** 1.8 **in the first field, replacing the first** 0 **as shown.**

6 **In the Variables category of commands, drag a** temperature (°C) **command to the workspace. Insert this command in the** 1.8 x 0 **command, replacing the** 0 **as shown.**

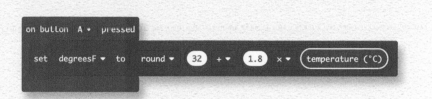

The code for measuring the temperature is done. The micro:bit reads the temperature in degrees Celsius, and your code converts this to degrees Fahrenheit.

7 **In the Basic category of commands, drag a** show number **command to the workspace. Attach this command to the previous command, inside** on button A pressed.

8 **In the Variables category of commands, drag a** degreesF **variable to the workspace. Insert this variable inside** show number.

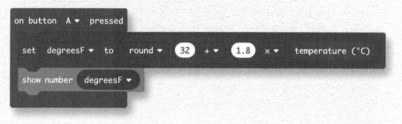

This completes the code for showing the temperature. The micro:bit scrolls the degreesF variable — the temperature read by the sensor and converted to Fahrenheit — on the LED display.

FUN WITH MATH

To convert a temperature in Celsius to Fahrenheit, multiply the Celsius temperature by 9/5 and then add 32. This is the same math you are doing in your code! (9/5 is the same as 1.8.) The computations follow the math order of operations, in which the multiplication by 1.8 takes places before the addition of 32. You then round your answer to get rid of decimal digits.

In MakeCode for micro:bit, you see all the code in the workspace. This differs from Scratch, where you can see only the code of the sprite or stage you're currently working on.

CONTINUE CODING BUTTON A TO SHOW IF THE POPS ARE FROZEN

You will use selection to tell the user if the pops are done. *Selection* means deciding on a path in your program. The basic code for selection is an if-then conditional command: *if* [condition is true] *then* [run this code]. Add the following to your program:

1 In the Logic category of commands, drag an if-then **command to the workspace and attach it to the previous command as shown.**

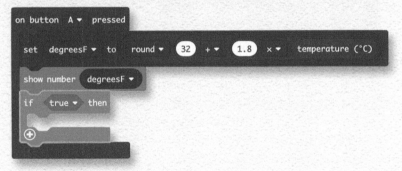

2 In the Logic category of commands, drag a 0 = 0 **command to the workspace and place it inside the** if **part of the** if-then **command (replacing** true**).**

Click the down arrow on the command tile and change the comparison to the greater than sign (>) so that the command reads 0 > 0.

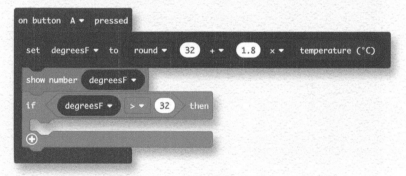

When dragging a command into another tile, you'll know you have the new command positioned correctly when the receiving area of the base tile lights up with a bright outline.

TIP

3 **In the Variables category of commands, drag a** degreesF **variable to the workspace. Insert this variable inside** 0 > 0, **replacing the first** 0. **Type the number** 32 **in the second field so that the command reads** if degreesF > 32 then.

You will now build the consequence of the conditional command.

4 **In the Basic category of commands, drag a** show string **command to the workspace. Insert this command inside the** then **of the** if degreesF > 32 then **command. Type** WAIT **in the** show string **field (MakeCode will add the quotation marks).**

```
on button  A ▾  pressed

  set  degreesF ▾  to   round ▾   32   + ▾   1.8   x ▾   temperature (°C)

  show number  degreesF ▾

  if      degreesF ▾   > ▾   32    then

    show string  "WAIT"

  ⊕
```

If the micro:bit thermometer reads a temperature of more than 32 degrees Fahrenheit — a value more than freezing — it scrolls the word *WAIT* on its screen.

5 **Repeat Steps 1 to 4 to make a second sequence. This new conditional should follow the previous** if-then **command and should read** if degreesF ≤ 32 then show string "FREEZE".

```
on button  A ▾  pressed

  set  degreesF ▾  to   round ▾   32   + ▾   1.8   x ▾   temperature (°C)

  show number  degreesF ▾

  if      degreesF ▾   > ▾   32    then

    show string  "WAIT"

  ⊕

  if      degreesF ▾   ≤ ▾   32    then

    show string  "FREEZE"

  ⊕
```

If the micro:bit thermometer reads a temperature of less than or equal to 32 degrees Fahrenheit — a freezing temperature — it scrolls the word *FREEZE* on its screen.

FUN WITH CODE

In coding, we say that the condition of an if-then is Boolean because the value is true or false.

SAVE, TEST, AND DEBUG YOUR PROGRAM

Click the Save button at the bottom of the screen to save your program in the cloud. (This also downloads your program.) Test your code by clicking the green play icon on the simulator. Press Button A and then drag the temperature line on the thermometer up and down to artificially change the temperature read by the micro:bit.

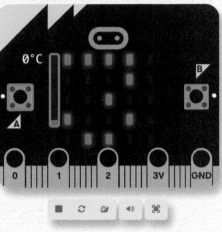

Each time you set the temperature on the simulator, press Button A again. The updated temperature in Fahrenheit scrolls on the screen followed by the word *WAIT* or *FREEZE* (depending on the temperature you set). Fix any bugs to make sure that your Freeze the Pops code works the way you want. (For help, see the section in Project 1 on debugging micro:bit programs.)

TRANSFER YOUR PROGRAM TO THE MICRO:BIT

After your code works the way you want it to on the simulator, you may choose to transfer it to a physical micro:bit. Plug your micro:bit into the USB port of your computer. Then drag the saved micro:bit hex file from your Downloads folder to the micro:bit icon on your desktop. The orange light on the back of the board will blink for a few seconds while the program transfers. After the program is on the micro:bit, you can detach the board from your computer's USB port. (For details on transferring programs to the micro:bit, see Project 7.) After you disconnect the micro:bit from your computer, attach the portable battery pack to the micro:bit.

TIP

Need an easy way to make freezer pops? Pour Kool-Aid into an empty ice tray and cover the tray with foil. Then, for each pop, poke a Popsicle stick through the foil and into the liquid.

PUT YOUR MICRO:BIT IN THE FREEZER

If you want, you can test your micro:bit in the real world. Make some liquid pops and place them in the freezer. Also place a zipped plastic bag, full of the same the liquid, in the freezer. Lay the micro:bit with the temperature sensor resting on the bag. (You are trying to measure the temperature of the liquid, not the air in the freezer.) Check your pops every half hour by opening the freezer and pressing Button A on your micro:bit.

When the micro:bit shows the word FREEZE, its thermometer is reading 32 degrees Fahrenheit or less. The temperature of the liquid in the bag may not have fully cooled to this temperature because the micro:bit also reads the temperature of the freezer air. Also, when a liquid cools to 32 degrees Fahrenheit, it still needs time to change from a liquid to a solid state. Your pops may need extra time to fully freeze!

TECHNICAL STUFF

ENHANCE YOUR GADGET

Wouldn't it be nice to check on the temperature of your ice pops without opening the freezer? You can! One cool option for doing this uses Bluetooth, allowing the physical micro:bit to send the temperature to your smartphone. You'll first have to add the Bluetooth services extension to your MakeCode dashboard.

TECHNICAL STUFF

Bluetooth uses a type of radio wave called UHF (ultra-high frequency) to send information without wires between devices over short distances.

bluetooth
Bluetooth services

Next, you add just a few new lines of code to tell your program to use Bluetooth. Then you install on your phone a free micro:bit companion app to monitor your micro:bit at a distance! Lastly, you pair your micro:bit with your phone — *pairing* means telling the physical devices that they will need to communicate with each other. Bluetooth should be able to work anywhere in your home or yard. If you want to try this, follow the guide available online at www.dummies.com/ gettingstartedwithcoding.

BIG IDEAS IN THE PROJECT

Event-driven programming: In an *event-driven program,* events affect how the program runs. An event can be a user action such as a button click. In this project, pressing Button A in the simulator, on the physical micro:bit, or in the companion app starts the program.

Input and output (I/O): *Input* means something put into a program and *output* means something that comes out of a program. In this project, the micro:bit thermometer gets input by reading the temperature. The LEDs give output by showing the temperature of the micro:bit and scrolling a message about the temperature.

Internet of Things (IoT): *IoT* is the world of everyday devices that connect and send data, such as home alarms, smart ovens, and sensor-enabled doggie doors. Wired and wireless communications systems connect technology devices. In this optional extension to this project, connecting devices by Bluetooth (a type of wireless communication system) lets you create an IoT gadget.

Math operations: *Math operations* mean doing math such as adding, subtracting, multiplying, dividing, or rounding. This project uses math operations to change the units of measurement for the temperature reading. Math operations follow standard rules of computation called *order of operations.*

Program selection: Computer code chooses a path based on what is happening in the program. Selection uses conditional (if-then) commands to set paths through the program. In this project, one message shows if the pops are not at a freezing temperature, and a different message shows if the pops are at a freezing temperature.

Thermometer sensor: A sensor that measures temperature. In this project, the micro:bit thermometer is used to sense the temperature of liquid in contact with the micro:bit.

Variable: A *variable* is a container that stores a value that can change. A variable can hold a string (such as text), a number, or a Boolean (true or false). In this project, the temperature variable holds the micro:bit thermometer reading in Celsius, and the degreesF variable holds the temperature reading in Fahrenheit.

PROJECT 4 JELLYFISH JUMBLE

OH NO, THE JELLYFISH ARE ALL JUMBLED UP — CAN YOU FIND THE REAL MR. JELLY?

In this project, you code a funny search-and-find puzzle featuring jellyfish on the ocean floor. First, you make a real Mr. Jelly. Then, by using *repetition* (doing something over and over), you make lots of *clones*, or copies, to create fakers. The fakers look just like Mr. Jelly — except, unlike Mr. Jelly, all the fakers are a little bit see-through! The fakers scatter to *random* places in the water — different places the computer creates for every puzzle — trying to confuse the player as she searches for Mr. Jelly. The player wins by finding and clicking the real Mr. Jelly. When Mr. Jelly is clicked, he announces, "You found me!" As you design and code your program, you add animation and sound effects to make the puzzle even more fun.

BRAINSTORM

In this project, you work in Scratch to create your own search-and-find puzzle for viewing on a computer or tablet. Your scene uses assets from the Scratch libraries. You can create any setting and characters you want! This project uses the *ghost* effect to make the faker jellyfish varying degrees of see-through, but you may choose to use the *color* effect to create fakers of slightly different colors.

FLOWCHARTS

Plan your Jellyfish Jumble program by drawing flowcharts to show how the program will run. The flowcharts don't need to have every step; include just the main parts.

When I think about my program, I know that I want to make jellyfish who live in the ocean. To do this, I need to add a Jellyfish sprite (Mr. Jelly) and another Jellyfish sprite (Fake, which I will clone to make additional fakers). Then I will write code that executes when the user clicks the green flag icon.

For this project, I need two flowcharts. One flowchart sets up the puzzle when the user clicks the green flag. The setup has different parts happening at the same time (in *parallel*).

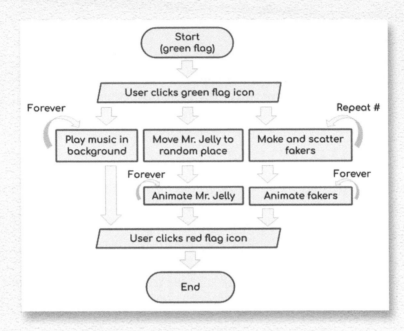

Here are the parts of the green flag flowchart:

» **In the background:** Loop ocean sounds until the program stops.

» **Mr. Jelly sprite:** Send the real Jellyfish sprite, Mr. Jelly, to a random location onscreen and animate him.

» **Fake jelly:** Fake makes and scatters more fakers onscreen. The fakers animate.

The second flowchart is for searching for Mr. Jelly and clicking him when you find him. If Mr. Jelly is clicked by a user, he lets the user know that he's been found. No message appears if the user clicks a faker. Here are the parts of the Mr. Jelly clicked flowchart.

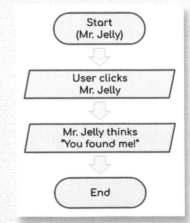

Now, get started coding your Jellyfish Jumble!

START A NEW PROJECT

Begin creating your Jellyfish Jumble program by starting a new project:

1 **Open Scratch at** `https://scratch.mit.edu`.

2 **On the Scratch home page, select Create.**

Or if you're already working in Scratch, choose File ⇨ New Project from the menu bar. A new project opens.

3 **Name your program by typing a name in the project name field at the top of the Scratch interface.**

I named my program `Jellyfish Jumble`.

4 **Cut (delete) Scratch Cat from the project by clicking or tapping the X in the Scratch Cat icon.**

You can find the icon in the sprite area in the lower-right corner of the Scratch dashboard.

ADD A BACKDROP

The *backdrop* is the background color or image that fills the screen of your game. Add a backdrop as follows:

1 **At the stage, click the choose a backdrop icon.**

The backdrop library appears on the Choose a Backdrop screen.

2 **From the list of backdrops, click or tap the backdrop you want.**

Your backdrop appears on the stage. I chose the Underwater 1 backdrop for my program.

ADD A JELLYFISH SPRITE AND CUSTOM COSTUMES

Your puzzle program has Jellyfish sprites, and each has costumes that you can change. Changing costumes over time animates the jellyfish, making them appear to swish their tentacles in the water.

Add a Jellyfish sprite to your scene and create its costumes by following these steps:

1 In the sprite area of the Scratch interface, click the choose a sprite icon.

The sprite library appears on the Choose a Sprite screen.

2 In the list of sprites, click or tap the sprite you want.

I picked Jellyfish. Your sprite appears on the stage.

3 **Click the Costumes tab to open the costume editor. Here, you can view all the costumes that come with the sprite.**

The tan costume is currently selected, but I will use only the white costume, which is named jellyfish-d by default. (I think it looks most like a jellyfish that once floated past me in the surf at Padre Island in Texas!)

4 **Cut the costumes you don't want to use by clicking the X in the corner of each costume icon.**

You should cut the tan, orange, and red costumes. These are named jellyfish-a, jellyfish-b, and jellyfish-c. This leaves only the white jellyfish costume.

5 **Duplicate the white costume by Control-clicking (Mac) or right-clicking (Windows) its icon and selecting Duplicate from the pop-up menu.**

You now have two white jellyfish costumes.

6 In the costume editor, on one of the costumes — it doesn't matter which one — click or tap the Ungroup button.

This ungroups the different body parts of the jellyfish so you can edit them individually.

7 Click a tentacle to select it and then edit its appearance and size.

Drag the tentacle to a slightly different position, drag a sizing dot to shrink or increase its size, or turn its rotation handle (or do all of these).

8 Repeat Step 7 to change the appearance of a few more tentacles.

The goal is to make the tentacles look a little different on the two costumes.

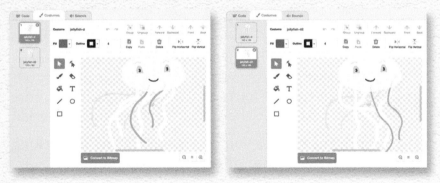

MAKE A MR. JELLY SPRITE AND A FAKE SPRITE

Now that you have a Jellyfish sprite that looks the way you want, you can use it to create the jellyfish characters for your puzzle. You will now make and name two sprites: Mr. Jelly and Fake. (Later, Fake will be cloned to make lots of fakers, also known as *distractors* — objects that make it hard for the user to find the real Mr. Jelly.)

1 **Continue working in the sprite area of the Scratch interface. Be sure you have the Jellyfish sprite selected.**

2 **Resize the Jellyfish sprite by typing a new number in the Size field above the sprite.**

The default (starting) size of a sprite is 100. I changed my jellyfish to size 40.

3 **Type a new name in the Sprite field.**

The default (starting) name is Jellyfish. I changed the name to Mr. Jelly.

4 **In the sprite area, Control-click (Mac) or right-click (Windows) Mr. Jelly and select Duplicate from the pop-up menu. Change the name of the duplicate Jellyfish sprite to Fake.**

Fake is an exact copy of Mr. Jelly — all the attributes, including costumes and size, are the same. (Don't worry about making Fake look different from Mr. Jelly — only the fakers need to look different because eventually you will hide Fake.) Both Jellyfish sprites, Mr. Jelly and Fake, now appear on the stage. An icon for each sprite also appears in the sprite area of the Scratch dashboard. The figure shows both Jellyfish sprites, sized and on the Underwater backdrop.

REMEMBER

If you add a sprite and then decide you don't want it, cut it by clicking or tapping the X in its icon.

Your user interface is now complete! The Jellyfish Jumble user interface has a stage with a backdrop and two Jellyfish sprites. You can click and drag the sprites to any position you like on the main stage — but the code you write later will move them to random positions anyway!

TECHNICAL STUFF

Scratch doesn't care what you name assets, variables, or new code blocks. But most other coding languages have rules about naming — they use camelCase naming. Like a camel, the name starts low (with a lowercase letter) and goes high (with an uppercase letter) each time you start a new word. So if you are naming a sprite, you could call it something like `mrJelly` *or* `fakeMrJelly`.

CODE THE GREEN FLAG BLOCKS

The green flag code sets up the puzzle. You will write green flag code for the backdrop and both sprites.

BACKGROUND

The backdrop plays music that loops until the user clicks the stop icon or finds Mr. Jelly. Here's how to code it:

1 **Select the backdrop by clicking its icon on the stage.**

2 **On the Code tab of the Scratch interface, select the Events category. Drag a** when green flag clicked **event command to the code workspace.**

The green flag command starts the code block.

3 **From the Control category, drag a** forever **loop command to the workspace and attach it to the previous command.**

Any command placed inside the loop will repeat forever.

4 **Select the Sound icon. Drag the** play sound until done **command to the code workspace and attach it to the previous command.**

5 **Click or tap the down arrow on the** play sound until done **command tile and select the sound you want for the background.**

I chose the Ocean Wave sound, which comes with the Underwater 1 backdrop.

The code block for the backdrop is now complete!

MR. JELLY

When a user clicks or taps the green flag, Mr. Jelly should go to a random location and animate. Write the code like this:

1 **Select Mr. Jelly by clicking his icon in the sprite area.**

2 **On the Code tab of the Scratch interface, select the Events category. Drag a** when green flag clicked **event command to the code workspace.**

The green flag command starts the code block.

3 **From the Motion category, drag a** go to random position **command to the workspace and attach it to the previous command.**

Now you will add a forever loop to give Mr. Jelly an animated swish. The swish will happen every second, when he changes between his two costumes.

1 **From the Control category, drag a** forever **loop command to the workspace and attach it to the previous command.**

Any command placed inside the loop will repeat forever.

2 **From the Control category, drag a** wait 1 seconds **command to the code workspace and attach it inside the** forever **loop.**

3 **From the Looks category, drag a** next costume **command to the code workspace and attach it to the previous command, inside the** forever **loop.**

Here is the final green flag code block for Mr. Jelly.

FAKE AND THE FAKERS

When a user clicks or taps the green flag, Fake goes into action. Fake uses a ghost effect to appear a little see-through, and then he clones to put a copy of himself in the water. Last, Fake moves to a new, random location in the water and repeats the ghosting and cloning. By doing ten repeat loops, Fake fills up the ocean with fakers. Write the code like this:

1 **Select Fake.**

2 **On the Code tab of the Scratch interface, select the Events category. Drag a when green flag clicked event command to the code workspace.**

3 **Select the Looks category. Drag a show command to the code workspace.**

The fake jellyfish must show (appear) before you can clone it. This matters only if it is hidden at some other time (which it is — as you see in a few steps).

4 **From the Control category, drag a repeat 10 loop command to the workspace and attach it to the previous command.**

Any commands placed inside the loop will be executed ten times. After the repeat loop, the code block will execute the next command in sequence.

5 **Select the Looks category. Drag a set color effect to 0 command to the code workspace, placing it inside the repeat loop. Press the down arrow on**

the command tile to reveal the pop-up menu of effect options.

6 **In the effects menu, change** color **to** ghost.

7 **From the Operations category, drag a** pick random **loop command to the workspace and place it inside the** set ghost effect **command, replacing the** 0. **Type numbers to change the range of the random command.**

You can change the random range to anything you want. I used pick random 10 to 20. Bigger numbers make the sprite more see-through. Here is the newly added ghost effect.

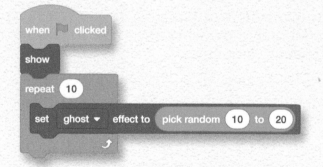

8 **From the Control category, drag a** create clone of myself **command to the workspace and attach it to the previous command, inside the** repeat **loop.**

This clones Fake, who is wearing a random ghost effect. The clone is created at the same position Fake is located. (The clone is "stacked on top" of Fake.)

9 **From the Motion category, drag a** go to random position **command to the workspace and attach it to the previous command, inside the** repeat **loop.**

This sends Fake to a new, random position. Fake leaves behind the clone he just made. The repeat loop is now complete.

10 **From the Looks category, drag a** hide **command to the workspace and attach it to the previous command.**

The hide command hides Fake after the repeat loop completes. (By hiding Fake, you don't have to write extra commands to animate him later.)

You're all finished writing the green flag code for Fake. Now you just need to write a bit more code to finish the entire project.

CODE THE FAKER CLONES TO SWISH

If you test your code so far, you'll see (after you get any bugs out!) that the puzzle setup mostly works. But you probably noticed that the only sprite swishing is

Mr. Jelly. You need to animate the clones so that they swish, too. To do this, you have to write a separate code block for just the clones. Each clone will execute a forever loop in which it waits a second and then changes its costume, over and over. Here's how to code it:

1 **Continue working on Fake. From the Control category, drag a** when I start as a clone **header to the workspace to start a new code block.**

2 **From the Control category, drag a** forever **loop command to the workspace and attach it to the previous command.**

3 **From the Control category, drag a** wait 1 seconds **command to the code workspace and attach it inside the** forever **loop.**

4 **From the Looks category, drag a** next costume **command to the code workspace and attach it to the previous command, inside the** forever **loop.**

The when I start as a clone code block for Fake is finished.

Instead of showing and hiding Fake, you could add this same forever block of code to Fake to make him swish. Note that you have to do one or the other — either show/hide the sprite or add the animation loop to the end of the sprite's code. If you don't, the sprite will show but it won't swish like the clones.

CODE MR. JELLY TO KNOW HE'S BEEN FOUND

Test your code again. You should see that the puzzle sets up correctly and that all the jellies onscreen (real and fake) are swishing. But if you find and click Mr. Jelly, nothing happens. You need to write a final block of code in which Mr. Jelly responds to being found and clicked (or tapped) by the user:

1 **Continue working on Mr. Jelly. From the Control category, drag a** when this sprite clicked **header to the workspace to start a new code block.**

2 **From the Looks category, drag a** think Hmm... for 2 seconds **command to the code workspace and attach it to the code block header. Change** Hmm... **to** You found me!

You can leave the 2 seconds as-is.

3 **From the Control category, drag a** stop all **loop command to the workspace and attach it to the previous command.**

After Mr. Jelly thinks aloud that he has been found, the entire program stops. This has the same effect as the user clicking the red stop icon.

The when this sprite clicked code block for Mr. Jelly is finished.

FUN WITH CODE

Building your program in chunks and testing as you go is called coding iteratively. When you iterate, you develop your program in stages, the way real coders do!

ENHANCE YOUR SCENE

Consider enhancing your puzzle with new features:

» **User-selected difficulty:** Instead of making ten fakers, the users can input the number they want. Use an ask command to ask the users how many fakers they want. Then, instead of using repeat 10 to create clones, replace the 10 with the user's answer. The ask and answer commands are in the Sensing category.

» **New sound:** Add new sounds from the sound library or that you record. For instance, you can make Mr. Jelly scream or make another funny sound when he's found. Just add a play sound until done command to Mr. Jelly's when this sprite clicked code block.

» **New sprite and sound:** Create an entirely different puzzle just by changing the characters and the setting!

» **New effect:** Instead of using a white jelly and the ghost effect, try using a colorful jelly and the color change effect!

» **Random sizing and random direction:** Instead of having all your sprites appear the same size and pointing in the same direction, use the random command to vary the sprite and clone attributes. You learn more about direction in Project 6.

Here is an example code snippet with a new effect, random sizing, and random direction that you can use to enhance your program. Note that a new scene and sprite are featured, too!

SAVE, TEST, AND DEBUG YOUR PROGRAM

As you work, Scratch automatically saves your program in the cloud, so you don't have to take any special actions to save your work. Test your program by clicking Mr. Jelly and also clicking some fakers to see the program's response. Fix any bugs to ensure that the entire program works the way you want it to. (For help with debugging, see the section in Project 1 on debugging Scratch programs.)

SHARE YOUR PROGRAM WITH THE WORLD

After your program operates perfectly, it's time to share it! Set the status of your program to Share, and then add to your project page a description of your program and directions on how to run it. See Project 7 for details on sharing your programs.

BIG IDEAS IN THE PROJECT

Cloning: *Cloning* means using an object (such as a sprite) to make identical copies of the object. The copies are called *clones*. The clones *inherits* (receives) all the attributes of the *parent* (original) object. These attributes can be changed later.

Event-driven programming: In an *event-driven program*, events affect how the program runs. An event can be a user action such as a button click. In Jellyfish Jumble, events are triggered by the user clicking the green flag, the program making faker clones, and the user clicking Mr. Jelly.

Iterate: *Iterate* means to code, test, and debug the code in stages, building up the completed program.

Parallel processing: When the computer program runs different blocks of code at the same time (in *parallel*), two or more things happen in your program at once. In Jellyfish Jumble, the green flag starts the execution of code blocks on the backdrop and both sprites, all at the same time. Other processes happen in parallel, too. For example, the background music continues looping forever while all the jellyfish swish.

Program sequence: Computer code runs one command after another, in order.

Random: In programming, a *random* number has different values each time you run your code. For toys, games, and puzzles, users want to have some variety as they play. Randomness creates that variety. In Jellyfish Jumble, you send the Jellyfish sprites to random places in the water. You use randomness also to ghost all the fakers by different amounts. When coding randomness, you set the range of values (usually, low to high) that your random number can have.

Repetition: Repetition, or *looping*, of computer code lets you make sections of your code run many times, without having to write that code over and over. You can create loops in different ways. In this project, you use a `forever` loop so that the animation keeps going and music keeps playing until the program stops. You also use a `repeat` loop to make a section of code repeat a known number of times. You use more repetition and different types of loops later in this book.

User interface (UI): The *user interface* is what users see onscreen and the way they use your program. The user interface in this project is a puzzle that shows a setting and funny characters. The users must click or tap the screen to play.

PROJECT 5 CARD WAR

YOU CODE A CLASSIC CARD GAME IN THIS MAKECODE FOR MICRO:BIT PROJECT! Card War pits two players against each other, with players holding their own micro:bit devices. Each player shakes his or her micro:bit to make a random number. Using radio waves, the micro:bits "talk" to each other to compare their numbers. The micro:bits then show who wins (the person with the higher number), who loses (the person with the lower number), or — in the event of a tie — war! In this project, you use two variables and work with an advanced form of selection called a conditional sieve. You also produce random numbers in a range that you set. Last, you work with an accelerometer sensor and code radio communication. An *accelerometer* senses whether the speed or direction of an object is changing. You can simulate the game on your computer, or — if you and a friend each have a micro:bit — you can make the physical game!

BRAINSTORM

In this project, you work in MakeCode to make your own electronic game. You use an accelerometer sensor to wait for a shaking motion. When the shake event happens, the micro:bit runs some code and sends some information by radio waves to another nearby micro:bit.

You can follow the directions for this project exactly to play the game on a computer — or you can make real gadgets for playing this Card War game. Or make a different type of game or gadget, one that does something else with a sensor and the radio. The accelerometer can tell whether the micro:bit board is shaken, lifted, dropped, or turned! What about an emoji alarm that shows a happy face when it's at rest but a sad face when it's moved? Remember, the radio sends the state of one micro:bit to a different micro:bit — friends receive each other's emojis. How about using the *magnetometer* sensor, which works like a compass, to read which way the micro:bit is pointed? You can use the magnetometer and radio communication to see what direction a buddy is facing, and he or she can see what direction you're facing, too. With these components, you can create an orienteering game!

FLOWCHARTS

Plan your Card War game program by drawing flowcharts to show how the program will run. The flowcharts don't need to have every step, just the main parts.

When I think about my program, I know that I want to make an electronic toy that lets me play the game of Card

War. To do this, I need two flowcharts, one for making random numbers and one for checking who wins.

In the first flowchart, the event that starts the action is a shake of the micro:bit. The accelerometer of the micro:bit senses the shake and makes the micro:bit show a random number on its LEDs. The shake also sends the random number to the other person's micro:bit. Here is the flowchart for shaking and picking a number.

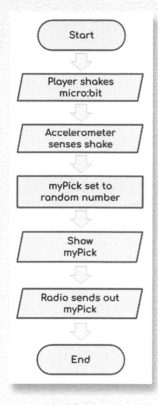

In the second flowchart, the event that starts the action is receiving a radio signal. When a micro:bit gets a number by radio, the micro:bit compares its own number with its opponent's number. The micro:bit then shows a symbol that tells who wins or loses (based on who has the bigger number). If both micro:bits have the same number, the micro:bit shows a symbol for a tie. This flowchart (shown on the next page) figures out who wins. Both micro:bits playing the game will follow the same instructions.

START A NEW PROJECT

Begin creating your Card War program by starting a new project:

1 **Open MakeCode for Micro:bit at** https://makecode.microbit.org.

2 **On the MakeCode home page, click the big purple New Project button.**

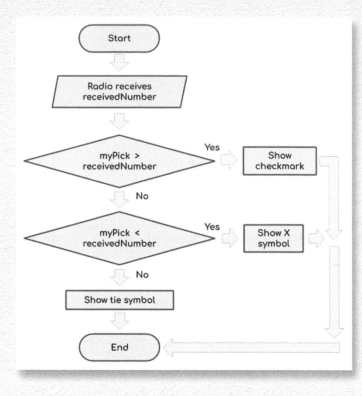

Or if you're already working in MakeCode, choose Home from the menu bar and then click the New Project button. A new project opens.

3 **Drag the** on start **and** forever **commands into the command categories area to recycle them — you won't need them.**

4 **Name your project by typing a name in the Project Name field at the bottom of the MakeCode dashboard.**

Keeping the name short, I named my project War, but you can name yours anything you want!

War   💾

5 **Click the Save button next to the Project Name field to save your project.**

MAKE A VARIABLE

Remember that a *variable* stores a value that can change. This project will have two variables. One variable is built into MakeCode. You need to make the other, a variable named myPick that holds a number representing the value of the card you draw from a deck of cards:

1 In the Variables category of commands, click the Make a Variable button.

2 In the New Variable Name dialog box, type the variable name myPick to store the value of a player's card.

> New variable name:
>
> myPick
>
> Ok ✔   Cancel ✖

3 Click OK.

The myPick variable is added to the list of variables you can use in your MakeCode project.

REMEMBER

In MakeCode for micro:bit, you see all the code in the workspace. This differs from Scratch, where you can see only the code of the sprite or stage you're currently working on.

CODE ON SHAKE TO MAKE AND SEND YOUR NUMBER

You build your code by dragging blocks into the MakeCode workspace. You will write an *event-driven* program to run when the micro:bit is shaken. (See Project 1 for help on event-driven programming.) Complete these steps:

1 **In the Input category of commands, drag an** on shake **command to the workspace.**

   When the end user shakes the micro:bit, it will run the code block (which you create in the next steps). The accelerometer sensor is the component that senses the change in movement of the micro:bit.

2 **In the Variable category of commands, drag a** set myPick **command to the workspace and drop it inside the** on shake **command.**

   The command shows a default value of 0. You'll replace this number in the next step.

3 **In the Math category of commands, drag a** pick random **command to the workspace. Insert this command in the** set myPick **command, replacing the 0.**

4 **Set the range of the** pick random **command from** 2 **to** 10 **by typing these numbers in the fields.**

This sets the value of the myPick variable to a random number from 2 to 10. These are the number values in a deck of cards, and we will play the Card War game with only these values. The face cards (Jack, Queen, King) and the Ace card will not be used.

5 **In the Basic category of commands, drag a** show number **command to the workspace. Attach this command to the previous command, inside the** on shake.

6 **In the Variables category of commands, drag a** myPick **variable and place it inside** show number. **The command now reads** show number myPick.

This command displays the value of the myPick variable, a number from 2 to 10, on the LED display.

7 **In the Radio category of commands, drag a** radio send number **command and attach it to the previous command, inside the** on shake.

8 **In the Variables category of commands, drag a** myPick **variable and place it inside** radio send number. **The command now reads** radio send number myPick.

This command uses a radio to send the value of the myPick variable to another nearby micro:bit.

The code for shaking the micro:bit to make, show, and send a random card number is complete! Both micro:bits follow the same rules.

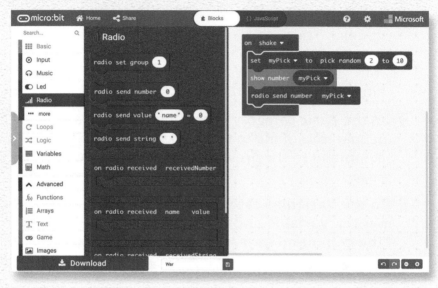

TECHNICAL STUFF

When using micro:bits, you can set a radio group so that the devices in the group "tune in" to each other — a little like tuning in a broadcast radio station. If you don't set a radio group, the micro:bits are set to the same group by default.

CODE AN ON RADIO RECEIVED BLOCK TO IDENTIFY A WINNER

You will create a new code block that figures out which of the two micro:bits playing Card War is the winner and which is the loser — or whether they tie. The radio receive event makes this code block run from another micro:bit. To *radio receive* means that a micro:bit gets (receives) information from another micro:bit that is sending out information. In this project, each micro:bit both sends and receives a radio signal:

1 **In the Radio category of commands, drag an** on radio received **command to the workspace.**

2 **In the Variable category of commands, drag a** receivedNumber **command to the workspace and drop it inside the** on radio received **header.**

The complete header reads on radio received receivedNumber. Using radio communication, a

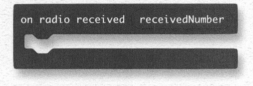

micro:bit will receive (get) a number from another micro:bit. The number it gets is receivedNumber (a built-in variable). When a micro:bit receives a signal by radio from another micro:bit, the code block inside the header runs.

In the next few steps, you will build the code block that runs when a micro:bit receives a number. You create this block as a type of selection command. (See Project 1 for help on selection.) The basic code for selection is this: *if* [a condition is true] *then* [run this code] *elseif* [a different condition is true] *then* [run this code] *else* [run this code as a last resort]. The *else* part tells your code what to do when all conditions are false.

3 **In the Logic category of commands, drag an** if-then-else **command to the workspace and attach it inside the code header.**

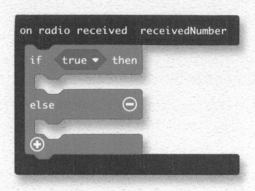

4 Click the plus (+) icon on the if–then–else command to expand it to an if–elseif–else command.

Yes — technically this looks like an if–then–elseif–then–else command — but that's too long to write, so computer programmers just refer to it by the nickname if–elseif–else.

TIP

When writing a conditional in MakeCode, click the plus (+) icon on a conditional to add new conditions to it, and click the minus (–) icon to remove conditions.

5 In the if condition of the if–elseif–else command, build a statement that reads if myPick > receivedNumber then:

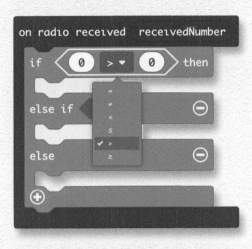

a. *From the Operations category, drag a* 0 < 0 *command to the code workspace and place it in the* if *condition, replacing* true. *(You know you're in the right place when the target area lights up with a yellow border.) Press the down arrow in the command and change* < *to* >.

b. *From the Variables category of commands, drag a* myPick *variable to replace the first* 0 *of* 0 > 0.

c. *From the* on radio received receivedNumber *command header, drag in the* receivedNumber *variable to replace the remaining* 0 *of* myPick > 0. *(Yes, it's weird that you have to "steal" a copy of this variable name from another command instead of finding it in the Variables category!)*

The code if myPick > receivedNumber then is now complete. This if statement checks whether the player's number (myPick) is greater than his or her opponent's number (receivedNumber). You will now build the then consequence that runs when the if condition is true.

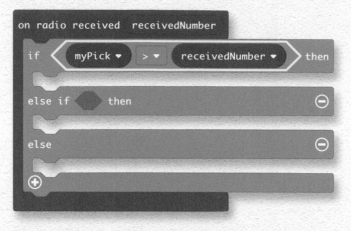

6 **In the** then **consequence of the** if-then **command, drag from the Basic category a** show icon **command. Click the down arrow in the command and select the checkmark icon from the menu.**

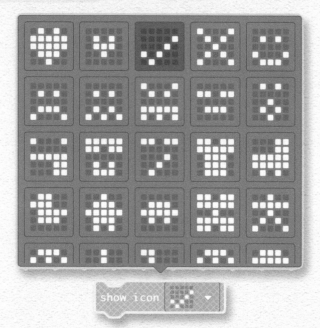

The then code for the show icon checkmark consequence is now complete. When players run a game of Card War, the checkmark icon is displayed on the micro:bit LEDs of the player with the larger number (that player who won). You will now build the elseif statement — both the condition and consequence.

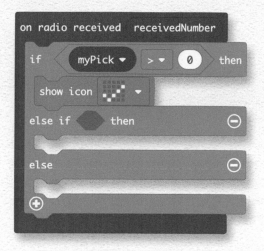

7 In the elseif **condition, build a statement that reads** if myPick < receivedNumber then **by repeating your actions in Step 5.**

8 In the then **consequence of the** elseif, **drag from the Basic category a** show icon **command. Click the down arrow in the command and select the** X **icon from the menu.**

When players run a game, the X icon will show on the micro:bit LEDs of the player with the smaller number (that player loses). Here's the code with the completed if and elseif conditionals.

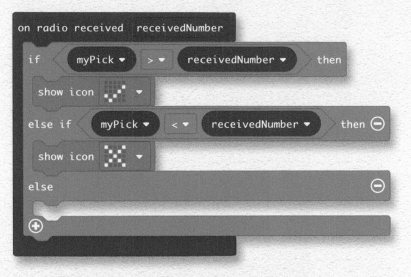

9 In the final `else` condition of the `if-then-else` command, drag from the Basic category a `show icon` command. Click the down arrow in the command and select from the menu the icon showing a small square.

When players run the game, the small square icon shows on the micro:bit LEDs when a player and his or her opponent tie (have the same card value in `myPick`).

TECHNICAL
STUFF

*The JavaScript code for the `show icon` checkmark command is `basic.showIcon`
(`IconNames.Yes`) — you can see this code if you click the toggle icon for JavaScript at the top of the MakeCode dashboard. The JavaScript commands for the other icon commands follow a similar pattern.*

Here is the complete program code for the game of Card War.

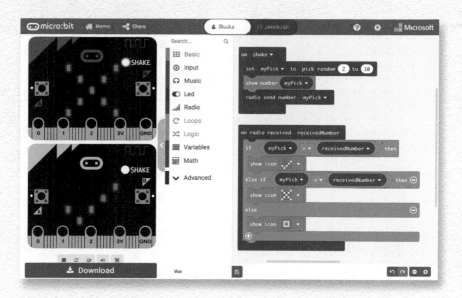

**FUN WITH
CODE**

*The `if–elseif–else` command lets you select
from many different paths to run. Putting
together a group of `elseif` statements lets you
make a conditional sieve. At the first condition
that is true, the associated consequence runs
and then the program exits the sieve. If nothing
"catches" — no condition is true — then the
final `else` statement (if there is one) executes.*

SAVE, TEST, AND DEBUG YOUR PROGRAM

Click the Save button at the bottom of the screen to save
your program in the cloud. Test your code by clicking
the green play icon on the simulator. Because this
program has radio communication between micro:bits,
you will see a second micro:bit appear in the simulator
when you click Play. In the simulator, click the Shake
buttons one after another as fast as you can to simulate
shaking two micro:bits at the same time. Each micro:bit

shows the shake and random number on the LEDs. After the numbers appear, the code determines and displays the winner and loser.

If both micro:bits show the same number, the code has the LEDs show the symbol for a tie.

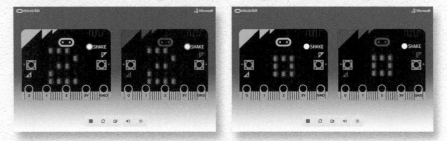

TECHNICAL STUFF

The zig-zag shaped radio transmitter symbol lights up in the top-right corner of the micro:bit image in the simulator when the micro:bit is sending or receiving information.

Fix any bugs to make sure that your Card War game code works the way you want. (For details, see the section on debugging micro:bit programs in Project 1.)

TRANSFER YOUR PROGRAM TO THE MICRO:BIT

After your code works the way you want it to on the simulator, you can transfer it to physical micro:bits. Because this game involves two micro:bits, you need to have two micro:bit boards. This section is optional, but it's a lot of fun to see your program running on actual micro:bits!

Plug each micro:bit, one at a time, into the USB port of your computer and then drag the saved micro:bit hex file from your Downloads folder to the micro:bit icon on your desktop. The orange light on the back of the board will blink for a few seconds while the program transfers. After the program is on the first micro:bit, detach the board from your computer's USB port, and then transfer the program to the second micro:bit. The program code must be transferred to both micro:bit boards. (For details on transferring programs to the micro:bit, see Project 7.) After you disconnect each micro:bit from your computer, attach a portable battery pack to each micro:bit.

ENHANCE YOUR GADGET

Try out new ways to use the accelerometer sensor! Instead of shaking the accelerometer, you can set the micro:bit to respond to another board motion, such as tilting, flipping, free fall, and vigorous (high g-force) moves. Just click the down arrow in the on shake command to set the event to a different sensor movement.

You can also set a different range of values for the random number command. For example, try something like 1 to 100. Or what about adding a sound to play when someone wins or loses? Just add a play tone or start melody command below each show icon command in the conditional sieve. (Note that the simulator will play the sounds, but to make the physical micro:bit produce sound, you need additional hardware — two alligator clips and a cheap external speaker or headphones for each micro:bit.)

BIG IDEAS IN THE PROJECT

Accelerometer sensor: An *accelerometer* is a sensor that detects a change in motion. In this project, the micro:bit accelerometer is used to sense a user shake.

Algorithm: An *algorithm* is a chunk of code that does a task. One algorithm in Card War is comparing numbers to determine a winner.

Event-driven programming: Events affect how the program runs. In this project, shaking the micro:bit starts the execution of a code block. Receiving a radio signal event starts the execution of a different code block.

Conditional sieve: A *conditional sieve* is a conditional that has several selection paths and is formatted if-elseif-else or something similar. When a true condition is reached, the consequence for that condition runs and the program exits the sieve. If no true condition is found, the else consequence executes.

Input and output (I/O): *Input* means something put into a program, and *output* means something that comes out of a program. In this project, the micro:bit accelerometer receives input by shaking and the radio antenna receives an input signal. The LEDs show output — the card value and whether a player wins, loses, or ties.

Program selection: Computer code chooses paths based on certain information. In this project, a conditional sieve is used to select one path: a player wins and the opponent loses, a player loses and the opponent wins, or they tie.

Radio communications: Like other gadgets in the *IoT (Internet of Things)* world, the Card War game in this project features a wireless communications system to connect technology devices. However, the IoT devices of this game use an older, simpler form of communication signal: *radio* communications. Radio messages are sent out by a *transmitter* and captured by a *receiver*. Radio is used for communicating relatively short distances and can be heard by many receiving devices at one time.

Random: Computer code often uses *random* numbers to create variation to simulate behavior in the real world. Random numbers usually have a range — in this project, the numbers are 2 to 10, representing the numbers on non-face cards in a deck of cards.

Variable: A *variable* is a holding container that stores a value. The values held by a variable can change. In this project, the myPick variable holds the random number representing a card in the game of Card War. The receivedNumber variable holds the number the micro:bit receives by radio from the opponent's micro:bit.

PROJECT 6 AVOID THE ASTEROIDS

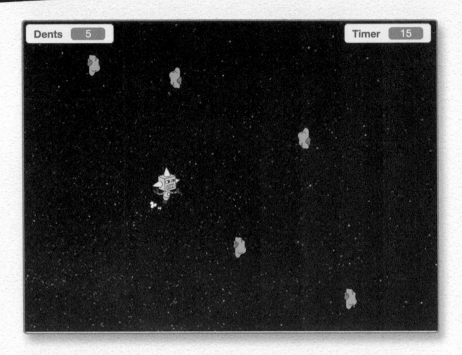

LITTLE ROBOTS LIKE TO PLAY SPACE GAMES, ESPECIALLY AVOID THE ASTEROIDS! In this project, you code a game in which the player moves a robot safely through an asteroid field. This final project puts together sequence, selection, and repetition as you write algorithms to control game action. It also introduces *coordinates* (the position of an object onscreen) to place the robot, direction to control where objects are headed, and key control for the user to move the robot. You'll *increment* (increase) a Dents variable when the robot and an asteroid *collide* (bump into each other). You'll *decrement* (decrease) a Timer variable to make the clock tick down to zero. And you'll use something new, a *logical* and command, to check the value of Dents *and* Timer to determine a win or a loss. Coding this game also introduces backdrop changes so that you can use an if-then-else conditional to display a special screen depending on how the user performs!

BRAINSTORM

In this project, you work in Scratch to create your own avoidance game for playing on a computer or a tablet. An *avoidance* game is one where the player must stay away from something. Your game uses assets from the Scratch libraries — I use deep space and a robot and asteroids, but you can use any setting and hero and obstacles. What about a muddy piglet avoiding water droplets from a bathtub? Or Superman avoiding Kryptonite? Dream up any story you want!

FLOWCHARTS

Plan your Avoid the Asteroids program by drawing flowcharts to show how the program will run. The flowcharts don't need to show every step; include just the main parts. This project has two flowcharts. One flowchart sets up the game and starts the action when the user clicks the green flag. A second flowchart describes the control of the robot.

When planning the game and mapping out your flowcharts, think about the assets you will have and use. For the game I'm making, I need three backdrops to display on the background — one for playing the game, one that shows when a player wins, and one that shows when a player loses. Then I'll create two sprites — a Robot sprite and an Asteroid sprite. Later, I'll duplicate the asteroid. Lastly, I'll make two variables: Dents, to count how many times the Robot collides with the asteroids, and Timer, to count down how much time the player has left.

GREEN FLAG FLOWCHART

The green flag flowchart maps what happens when the user clicks the green flag. This flowchart shows the setup and the game action. It has different code sequences happening at the same time (in parallel). Here are the parts of the green flag flowchart:

» **On the background:** Show the play backdrop. Play space sounds in a loop until the program is stopped. Set the Dents variable to 0 and set the Timer variable to 20. Make Timer count down to 0.

» **Robot sprite:** Send the Robot sprite to its starting place onscreen. Use a wait until conditional to check if the Robot sprite has reached the other side of the screen. If it has, check whether he had a safe run based on the values of the Dents and Timer variables. Set the win or lose backdrop and then stop the game.

» **Asteroid (rock) sprites:** The game has five identical Asteroid sprites. Each starts moving at a different time. Then they all move up and down the screen. If an Asteroid hits the Robot, the Dents variable is incremented by 1 — another way to write this is Dents ++.

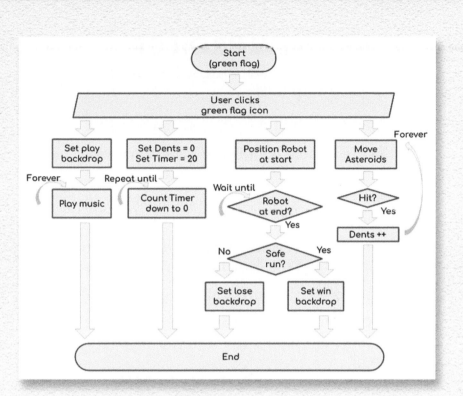

ROBOT FLOWCHART

Next is the flowchart for moving the Robot sprite. When the user presses the left arrow key, the Robot sprite moves to the left onscreen. When the user presses the right arrow key, the Robot sprite moves to the right onscreen.

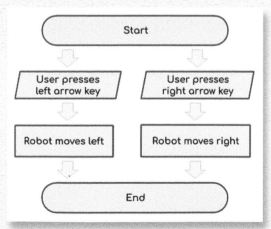

START A NEW PROJECT

Begin creating your Avoid the Asteroids program by starting a new project:

1 Open Scratch at https://scratch.mit.edu.

2 On the Scratch home page, select Create.

Or if you're already working in Scratch, choose File ⇨ New Project from the menu bar. A new project opens.

3 Name your program by typing a name in the project name field at the top of the Scratch dashboard.

I named my program Avoid the Asteroids.

4 Cut (delete) Scratch Cat from the project by clicking or tapping the X in the Scratch Cat icon.

ADD THREE BACKDROPS

You need three backdrops for your game: one for playing the game, one that shows when a player wins the game, and one that shows when a player loses. Add the backdrops as follows:

1 At the stage, click the choose a backdrop icon.

The backdrop library appears.

2 From the list of backdrops, click or tap the backdrop you want for your game play screen.

Your backdrop appears on the stage. I chose Stars, as shown in the opening figure of this project.

3 Repeat Steps 1 and 2, selecting the backdrop you want for your win screen.

Your backdrop appears on the stage. I chose Nebula.

4 In the backdrop editor, click the Text tool and type a message such as YOU WIN! on the Nebula backdrop. You can set the color and font by using the selectors in the backdrop editor. Pull the sizing dots to resize the text.

5 Repeat Steps 1 and 2, selecting a backdrop you want for your lose screen.

Your backdrop appears on the stage. I chose Moon.

6 In the backdrop editor, click the Text tool and then type a message such as TRY AGAIN on the Moon backdrop. Set the color and font and then pull the sizing dots to resize the text.

7 **Cut (delete) the default backdrop1 from the project by clicking or tapping the X in its icon.**

You can find the icon in the Backdrops tab area.

Now, only the three backdrops for your game appear on the Backdrops tab. The backdrop with its icon selected is the one that shows on the main stage. Right now, this should be the Stars backdrop. You will use this backdrop as you design the game play screen in the next few sections.

ADD A ROBOT SPRITE

Your game program has a Robot sprite. Add it to your program by following these steps:

1 **In the sprite area of the Scratch interface, click the choose a sprite icon.**

The sprite library appears.

2 **In the list of sprites, click or tap the sprite you want.**

I picked Robot. Your sprite appears on the stage.

3 Click the Costumes tab to open the costume editor.

You see all the costumes that come with Robot. I will use only the third costume, robot-c. This costume is facing in the direction that the sprite will be moving.

4 Select the robot-c costume by clicking it.

5 In the sprite attributes area, edit the name, size, and direction of the Robot sprite.

The default name of Robot can remain as is. The Robot sprite needs to be a bit smaller, so type a new size — 30 works well. The default direction of 90 faces the Robot to the right — you can leave this as is.

WARNING

Don't cut the unused costumes! Later, you can extend your project by animating your Robot sprite with the extra costumes.

ADD AN ASTEROID SPRITE

Your game program has Asteroid sprites. For now, add just one Asteroid sprite to your program by following these steps:

1 **In the sprite area of the Scratch interface, click the choose a sprite icon.**

The sprite library appears.

2 **In the list of sprites, click or tap the sprite you want.**

I chose Rocks, which is the most asteroid-looking sprite I could find. Your sprite appears on the stage.

3 **In the sprite attributes area, edit the name, size, and direction of the Rocks sprite.**

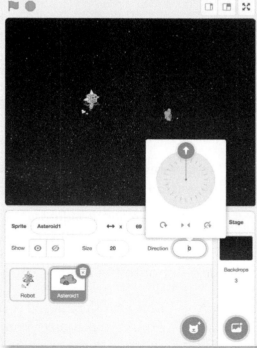

In the Sprite name field, change the name from Rocks to Asteroid1. (Later, after you code Asteroid1, you'll duplicate this sprite and number the new asteroids 2, 3, 4, and 5.) The Asteroid1 sprite needs to be much smaller, so type a new size such as 20. In the direction field, type 0

(or drag the direction dial to point to 0) so that the Asteroid1 sprite faces the top side of the screen.

Your user interface is now complete! The Avoid the Asteroids user interface has a stage with three backdrops and two sprites. Don't worry about the position of the sprites right now.

FUN WITH MATH

To point the sprite in a different direction, use the `point in direction` *command followed by a number: 0 points up, 90 points right, 180 points down, and 270 points left. To turn the sprite based on its current direction, use* `turn right` *or* `turn left` *followed by the angle (the number of degrees) that you want the sprite to turn. Use 90 for a hard right or hard left, and 180 to point the sprite in the opposite direction.*

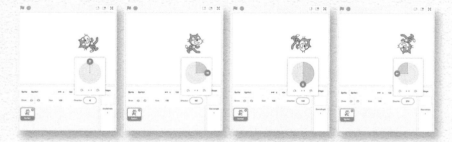

TECHNICAL STUFF

See the icons below the dial? When you point a sprite in a particular direction, you can choose the rotation style of the costumes (how you want the sprite to face). The all around icon (circle arrow) matches the direction. The left/ right icon (mirror-image arrows) means the user sees the object facing in the direction it is heading when it is moving left or moving right, but the object will never flip upside-down. The do not rotate icon (circle arrow with the line) means the sprite costume never rotates.

MAKE DENTS AND TIMER VARIABLES

In this project, you want to make two variables. Dents measures the number of collisions between the Robot and the Asteroids. The Timer ticks away seconds to encourage the player to get through the asteroid field quickly. Makes these variables as follows:

1 In the Variables category of commands, click the Make a Variable button.

2 In the dialog box, type the variable name Dents for the hits you will measure.

3 Press OK.

The Dents variable is added to the list of variables you can use in your project.

New Variable ✕
New variable name:
Dents
This variable will be available to all sprites.
Cancel   OK

Leave the checkbox next to Dents selected — this means that the variable will appear in an onscreen readout in your game. Drag the variable readout to a corner of your game on the main stage.

4 Repeat Steps 1 to 3 to create another variable called Timer.

Now, both the Dents and Timer variables show in the list of variables you can use in your project, and the variable readouts appear on the main stage.

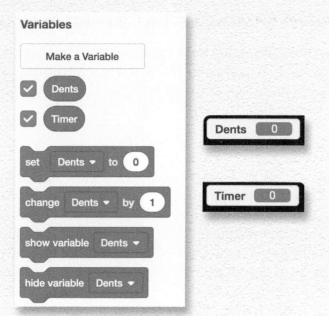

ADD BACKGROUND MUSIC FROM THE SOUND LIBRARY

Video games usually have background music playing as the user moves through the game. Add background music to your game as follows:

1 In the small stage area, click Backdrops. On the left side of the Scratch dashboard, switch to the Sounds tab.

2 Click or tap the choose a sound icon.

3 In the sound library, click or tap a sound you want to add to the background.

I clicked the Loops category and listened to the available sounds. Then I picked the Dance Space sound. Your selected sound is added to the Sounds tab for the backdrops.

CODE THE GREEN FLAG BLOCKS

The green flag code sets up the game. In this section, you write green flag code for the background — which includes any backdrop showing in the background — and the sprites.

BACKGROUND

When the game starts, the Stars backdrop is displayed, and then the music track starts playing and loops forever until the game ends. At the same time, the variables are *initialized* (set to their starting values) and then, as the game is played, the Timer counts down until it reaches 0. Because you have two repeat loops running in parallel — the music loop and the countdown loop — you will code *two* green flag blocks on the background.

Here's how to code the first green flag code block, for setting the backdrop and playing the music:

1 **Select the backdrop icon.**

2 **On the Code tab of the Scratch interface, select the Events category. Drag your first** when green flag clicked **event command to the code workspace.**

3 **From the Looks category, drag the** switch backdrop to Stars **command to the workspace and attach it to the code header.**

Press the down arrow in the command to change the backdrop. When the game starts, you want the Stars backdrop to show because it is where the player will play the game.

4 **Select the Control category. Drag the** forever **loop command to the code workspace and attach it to the previous command.**

Any commands placed inside the loop will repeat forever until the game ends.

5 **Select the Sound category. Drag the** `play sound until done` **command to the code workspace and attach it inside the** `forever` **command.**

6 **Click or tap the tab on the** `play sound until done` **command and select the sound you want to play in the background of the game.**

I chose the `Dance Space` sound.

The first green flag code block for the background is now complete!

Now you'll code the second green flag code block for the background:

```
when [flag] clicked
switch backdrop to   Stars ▼
forever
    play sound   Dance Space ▼   until done
```

1 **Still working on the backdrop, drag your second** `when green flag clicked` **event command from the Events category to the code workspace to start a new code block.**

2 **From the Variables category, drag a** `set Dents to 0` **command to the workspace and attach it to the code block header.**

You initialize `Dents` to 0 because Robot should have no dents (collisions) before he enters the asteroid field.

3 **Drag another** `set variable to 0` **command to the workspace and attach it to the previous command. Change the command to read** `set Timer to 20`.

You'll need to press the down arrow in the command and select the variable Timer. Type the number 20 (or however many seconds you want) in the field. You initialize Timer to 20 so that the player knows that he or she is trying to move through the asteroid field in this time period.

4 From the Control category, drag a repeat until **loop command to the workspace and attach it to the previous command.**

Any commands placed inside the loop will repeat until the condition of the repeat until is true.

5 Build a command that reads repeat until timer = 0 **as follows:**

a. *From the Operations category, drag an = command to the code workspace and attach it inside the* repeat until *loop.*

b. *From the Variables category, drag a* Timer *variable to the code workspace and attach it inside the first field of the = command.*

c. *Type the number 0 inside the second field of the = command.*

6 From the Control category, drag a wait 1 seconds **command to the workspace and attach inside the loop.**

7 From the Variables category, drag a change variable **command to the workspace and attach to the previous command, inside the loop. Change the command to read** change Timer by -1.

You'll need to press the down arrow in the command and select the variable Timer. Type the number -1 in the field. This command *decrements* (decreases) the Timer by 1, and it executes every 1 second (because of the previous command).

The second green flag code block for the background is now complete!

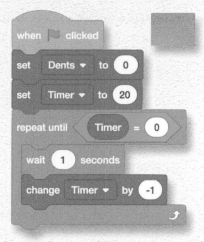

ROBOT

When a user clicks or taps the green flag, the Robot sprite should go to its starting location. As the user plays, the code should repeatedly check whether the user has reached the other side of the screen. Write the code like this:

1 Select the icon for the Robot sprite.

2 On the Code tab of the Scratch dashboard, select the Events category. Drag a when green flag clicked **event command to the code workspace.**

3 From the Motion category, drag a go to x: y: **command to the workspace and attach it to the previous command.**

This command lets you tell the sprite a *coordinate* — a location onscreen — to go to. A coordinate is a point and is defined by an *x position* (left-to-right) and a *y position* (bottom-to-top). To find the starting coordinate for the Robot sprite, drag it to the position you want, and then look at the x and y values in the sprite attributes area. You want to start the game with Robot at the far left and middle of the screen — this coordinate is x: −210 y: 0. Type these numbers in the fields.

Now you will add a loop that continually checks whether Robot has reached the right side of the screen, which means the player has passed through the asteroid field.

FUN WITH MATH

Every coding dashboard uses a coordinate system to show where things are onscreen. The x positions tell where an object is horizontally (left to right) on the screen, along the x-axis. The y positions tell where an object is vertically (bottom to top), along the y-axis. In Scratch, the center of the stage is at (0, 0). Scratch x positions go from −240 at the left of the stage to 240 at the right. Scratch y positions go from −180 at the bottom edge of the stage to 180 at the top edge.

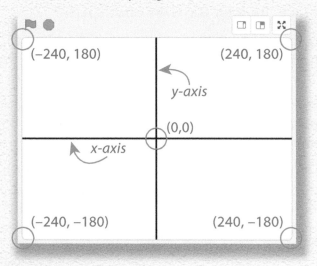

4 **From the Control category, drag a** wait until **command to the workspace and attach it to the previous command.**

The code for the Robot "sits and waits" here until the condition of the wait until is true.

5 **Build a command that reads** wait until x position > 200 then **as follows:**

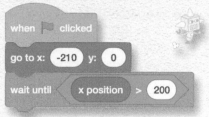

a. *From the Operations category, drag a* > *command to the code workspace and attach it inside the* if *of the* if then *loop.*

b. *From the Motion category, drag an* x position *command to the code workspace and attach it inside the first field of the* > *command.*

c. *Type the number 200 inside the second field of the* > *command.*

This command checks whether the user has moved Robot to an x-coordinate that is more than 200 — a location near the far right side of the main stage. The location is past where all the Asteroids will be flying. When the player gets the Robot sprite to this position, the wait is over and the next lines of code will execute.

You will now build the next lines of code.

FUN WITH CODE

JavaScript uses a different coordinate system than Scratch. In JavaScript, (0, 0) is at the top-left corner of the screen, and all coordinates are positive numbers.

6 **From the Control category, drag an** if-then-else **command to the workspace and attach it to the previous command.**

This code executes after the player has cleared the Asteroid field.

7 **From the Operations category, drag an** and **command to the code workspace. Attach the** and **inside the** if**.**

Two statements will be connected by the and. (You do that next.) Both statements must be true for the whole if condition to be true.

8 **Build the command** Dents < 10 **inside the first field of the** and **as follows:**

a. *From the Operations category, drag a < operator into the field.*

b. *From the Variables category, drag in a Dents variable and type the number 10 to complete the inequality.*

9 **Build the command** Timer > 0 **inside the second field of the** and**:**

a. *From the Operations category, drag a > operator into the field.*

b. *From the Variables category, drag in a Timer variable and type the number 0 to complete the inequality.*

The Robot will have to be dented less than ten times and there will have to be at least one second left on the Timer for the player to win the game.

The command now shows: if Dents < 10 and Timer > 0 then.

Logical operators are and, or, and not commands. Use a logical operator when your program needs to make a decision based on more than one condition. The and operator means that all conditions are true for the entire condition to be true. The or operator means that when any condition (one or more) is true, the entire condition is true. The not operator turns a true condition false, and a false condition true.

10 **From the Looks category, drag a** switch backdrop to **command to the code workspace and attach it inside the** then **of the** if-then-else **command. Press the down arrow in the command and select the** Nebula **backdrop from the list.**

The Nebula backdrop is the winning backdrop.

11 **Select the Sound category. Drag the** play sound until done **command to the code workspace and attach it to the previous command, inside the** then.

Click the down arrow on the play sound until done command and select the computer beep sound, which comes with the Robot sprite.

12 **From the Looks category, drag a** switch backdrop to **command to the code workspace and attach it inside the** else **of the** if-then-else **command. Press the down arrow in the command and select the** Moon **backdrop from the list.**

The Moon backdrop is the losing backdrop.

13 **From the Control category, drag a** stop all **command to the workspace and attach it to the previous command, inside the** then.

This command ends the execution of the code, so it ends the game.

Here is the final green flag code block for Robot.

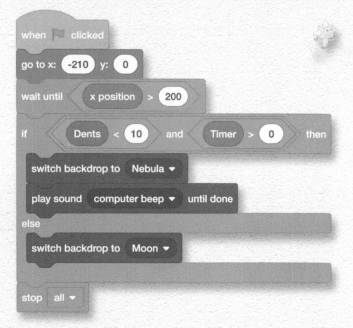

WARNING

Watch where you put that stop all *command! A common bug occurs when new coders place* stop all *outside the conditional. This causes* stop all *to execute almost immediately in the program, and all game action stops!*

ASTEROIDS

When a user clicks or taps the green flag icon, the asteroids move and bounce. If one hits Robot, the Dents variable increments by 1. Right now, you have just Asteroid1. You'll write code for this asteroid and then duplicate it later. Code Asteroid1 like this:

1 **Select the icon for the Asteroid1 sprite.**

2 **On the Code tab of the Scratch interface, select the Events category. Drag a** when green flag clicked **event command to the code workspace.**

3 **From the Control category, drag a** `wait` **command to the workspace and attach it to the previous command.**

4 **From the Operators category, drag a** `pick random` **command to the workspace and attach it inside the** `wait` **command. Type** 0 **and** 3 **so that the command reads** `wait random 0 to 3 seconds`.

This command varies the time at which the asteroid starts moving.

5 **From the Control category, drag a** `forever` **loop command to the workspace and attach it to the previous command.**

6 **From the Motion category, drag a** `move 10 steps` **command to the code workspace and attach it inside the** `forever` **loop.**

This sets Asteroid1 in motion. If you want the asteroid to move slower or faster, type a different number for the steps. Note that because you previously set the direction of Asteroid1 to 0, it points toward the top of the screen. When Asteroid1 starts moving on the first game play, it moves up the screen.

7 **From the Motion category, drag an** `if on edge, bounce` **command to the code workspace and attach it to the previous command, inside the** `forever` **loop.**

When Asteroid1 reaches the top edge of the screen it bounces. To *bounce* means to change direction 180 degrees and keep moving forward.

Here is the code so far — it includes all commands for launching, moving, and bouncing Asteroid1.

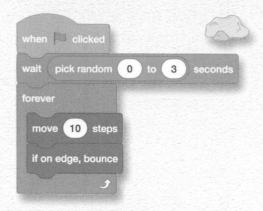

When an Asteroid and Robot collide, he gets a dent! Count these by incrementing the Dents variable by 1 after each collision. Write the code like this:

1 **Continue building onto the code block you have been writing for Asteroid1. From the Control category, drag an** if-then **conditional command to the workspace and attach it to the previous command, inside the** forever **loop.**

   This if-then conditional will run after each time the asteroid moves (and possibly bounces).

2 **From the Sensing category, drag a** touching **command to the code workspace and attach it inside the** if **of the** if-then **conditional. Press the down arrow and select** Robot.

   This command now reads if touching Robot? then. The conditional is checking whether this Asteroid sprite is colliding with the Robot sprite.

3 **From the Sound category, drag a** play sound pop until done **command to the code workspace and attach it to the previous command, inside the** then **of the** if-then **loop.**

   The pop sound comes with the Asteroid sprite and is what you might hear if a robot were dinged by a small asteroid.

4 **From the Variables category, drag a change Dents by 1 command to the code workspace and attach it to the previous command, inside the then of the if-then loop.**

This increments the Dents variable by 1 when a collision takes place. (A shortcut way to say this is Dents++.)

Here is the complete code for Asteroid1.

BUILD YOUR ASTEROID FIELD

Building your asteroid field is easy! You just need to duplicate Asteroid1 a few times and then position all the asteroid sprites. Follow these steps:

1 **Select the icon for the Asteroid1 sprite.**

2 **Duplicate Asteroid1 by Ctrl-clicking (Mac) or right-clicking (Windows) on the sprite icon in the sprites area and then clicking the Duplicate option from the menu that appears.**

A new Asteroid sprite is made and automatically named Asteroid2. The new sprite contains all the code of the original Asteroid sprite.

3 **Repeat Steps 1 and 2 to make Asteroid3, Asteroid4, and Asteroid5.**

4 **Drag the asteroids to the bottom of the stage, evenly spacing them apart.**

Give the Robot a little extra room on the left and right sides of the stage so that he doesn't get hit before entering the asteroid field or when leaving the asteroid field.

CODE KEY CONTROL OF THE ROBOT

Key control allows the user to press keys on the keyboard to move the Robot sprite through the asteroid field. To code key control, follow these steps:

1 **Click the Robot sprite icon in the sprite area.**

2 **From the Events category, drag a** when key pressed **command to the workspace to start a new code block. Press the down arrow in the command and set the key to** left arrow.

3 **From the Motion category, drag a** change x by 10 **command to the workspace and attach it to the previous command. Change the value from** 10 **to** –10.

When the user presses or taps the left arrow key, the Robot sprite changes its x position by –10. Changing a negative amount means moving left, so Robot moves left by 10 pixels.

4 **From the Events category, drag a** when key pressed **command to the workspace to start a new code block. Press the down arrow in the command and set the key to** right arrow.

5 **From the Motion category, drag a** change x by 10 **command to the workspace and attach it to the previous command.**

When the user presses or taps the right arrow key, the Robot sprite changes its x position by 10. Changing a positive amount means moving right, so Robot moves right by 10 pixels.

The arrow key control code is now complete!

ENHANCE YOUR SCENE

Consider enhancing your game with new features:

» **New sounds and animation:** Add new sounds and animated movements to your program. For instance, you can animate Robot by using his built-in extra costumes and adding next costume commands to the user key-control code blocks. You can also add sounds to the key-control blocks to help create the effect of Robot zooming through space — consider using one or more of the extra sounds that come with Robot!

» **New sprite and sounds:** Create an entirely different game experience just by changing the characters and the setting.

» **Random sizing:** Instead of having all your Asteroid sprites the same size, use the random command and the set size command to vary their size.

SAVE, TEST, AND DEBUG YOUR PROGRAM

As you work, Scratch automatically saves your program in the cloud, so you don't have to take any special action to save your work. Test your program by clicking the green flag and by using the arrow keys to see the program's response. Fix any bugs to ensure that the entire program works the way you want it to. (For help, see the section in Project 1 on debugging Scratch programs.)

SHARE YOUR PROGRAM WITH THE WORLD

After your program operates perfectly, it's time to share it. Set the status of your program to Share, and then add to your project page a description of your program and directions on how to run it. See Project 7 for details on sharing your programs.

BIG IDEAS IN THE PROJECT

Algorithm: An *algorithm* is a chunk of code that does a task. One algorithm in Avoid the Asteroids is moving and bouncing the asteroids forever.

Collision: A *collision* occurs when two objects are located at the same place onscreen. Being located at the same place means the objects (sprites) share the same (x, y) coordinates or that part of one sprite shares the same coordinates as part of another sprite. Checking for collisions, by using the touching command, lets you tell when two objects have bumped into each other.

Decrement: *Decrement* means to decrease (make smaller) the value of a variable.

Event-driven programming: In an *event-driven program*, events affect how the program runs. An event can be a user action such as a button click or a keypress. In Avoid the Asteroids, events are triggered by the user clicking the green flag, the user pressing arrow keys, and the value of variables determining a loss or a win.

Increment: *Increment* means to increase (make bigger) the value of a variable.

Input and output (I/O): *Input* means something put into a program and *output* means something that comes out of a program. In this project, the user uses keypresses to provide direction input to the Robot sprite. The game provides output by moving Robot left or right.

Key control: Computer keyboard control can be used to control objects onscreen in a video game. The arrow keys and the A, W, S, and D keys are frequently used to move a character around, and the spacebar is sometimes used for shooting or launching in a game. In Scratch, the when key pressed command serves as an event to make a sprite move.

Logical operator: *Logical operators,* such as and, or, and not, let you code your program to make a decision based on more than one condition. This program uses the and operator to make sure that the player clears the asteroid field quickly and with few dents to win the game.

Parallel processing: This term means that the computer program runs different blocks of code at the same time (in *parallel*), so you can have more than one thing happening in your program at once. In this game, many different commands are executed in parallel.

Position and direction: *Position* is the location onscreen where an object is located. Position is usually shown as an (x, y) coordinate telling where the object is left to right and bottom to top on the stage. *Direction* is which way an object is pointed. Direction is shown as a number from 0 to 360, going around a circle clockwise.

Program sequence: Computer code runs one command after another, in order.

Program selection: Computer code chooses paths based on certain information. Selection uses conditionals including if-then, if-then-else, and wait until commands to pick and control paths through the program.

Random: *Randomness* means making values in your code change unpredictably each time you run the code. In this game, random wait times create variation in the launching of the Asteroids.

Repetition: Using repetition in your code allows you to make sections of your code run over and over. In this project, you use a forever loop to make some processes continue until the program stops. You also use a repeat loop to repeat a section of code a known number of times. And you use a repeat until loop to decrement the Timer until it reaches 0.

User interface (UI): The *user interface* is the way a person uses your program. The user interface in this project is a game that has a setting, characters, a goal, key control, and a way to lose or win.

Variable: A *variable* is a holding container that stores a value. In this project, Dents stores the number of collisions between Robot and the Asteroid sprites, and Timer counts down how many seconds remain in a game run.

PROJECT 7 GET FANCY

NOW THAT YOU'VE LEARNED SOME CODING BASICS, I HOPE YOU WANT TO DO EVEN MORE CODING! You've seen that coding lets you take ideas and turn them into real apps and gadgets. So where do you go from here? Read on. This last project is a lot of little pieces that will help you take the next steps in coding.

You'll explore how you can spark your own ideas for coding new creations. You'll learn how to share your projects (if you want to) and find other people who are learning to code, like you. You'll discover the easy steps for putting your MakeCode project code onto a real micro:bit and for adding electronic extras such as speakers. And you'll see some new resources for getting fun new assets for your projects, from sounds and graphics to 3D-printed add-ons. Last, you'll find out how to further develop your coding skills — no matter what you set as your goal, support is out there to help you level up. Keep reading to find out more!

PROGRAMMING YOUR OWN IDEAS

Sometimes, it's tough to imagine something you want to create with code. The key to getting started is to design and code something small. Starting a program gives you a real thing you can see and touch, something you can build on. You can finish the program or you can take it in a new direction. But at least you'll have done something! Here are some ways for getting creative and getting underway.

GETTING INSPIRATION FROM SCRATCHERS

By clicking the See Inside button on the project page of any Scratch project, you can see the code and assets used to make the program. This is a great way to learn and grow your understanding of the many creative things you can code. You'll be amazed at the programs that other *Scratchers* (Scratch programmers) have coded and shared in the Scratch *studios*, which are collections of projects for everyone to use. To see Scratch studios, click the Scratch logo (in the upper-left corner), click Explore, and then select Studios.

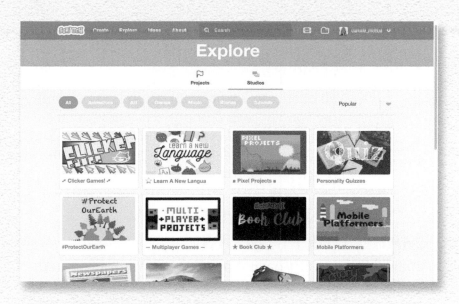

If you find a project you love, you can remix it. *Remixing* means starting with a project shared by another Scratcher and then changing it to make it your own, adding new graphics and new snippets of code. Sometimes, starting with an example project can help relieve the stress of trying to create something from the nothing of a blank screen.

TIP

You can also comment on a project, click the heart icon to like the project, and click the star icon to make it a favorite. The eyeball icon shows the number of project views.

To remix a project made by another Scratcher, click the Remix button at the top right of a project page. A copy of the project is then added to your My Stuff folder, for you to modify however you want. An *attribution* — a thank-you to the original coder— is added to your copy. Other Scratchers can remix your projects, too. The number of remixes of your project is shown next to the spiral symbol on your

Ⓖ **Remix**

project page. To see all remixes of your project, click View All in the Remixes area of your project page (in the bottom-right corner).

You can access any of your projects — original ones you've created or projects you've remixed from other Scratchers — by clicking the My Stuff icon (the little folder in the upper right of the Scratch dashboard).

REMEMBER

GETTING INSPIRATION FROM MAKECODE PROJECTS

MakeCode doesn't have a public collection of shared projects made by other people. But MakeCode's Ideas page at https://microbit.org/ideas provides some great material that might spark your creativity. Another good place to get tutorials and example projects is the MakeCode home page at https://makecode.microbit.org. You can reach this home page also by clicking the Home button at the top left of the workspace when working in any MakeCode project. In addition to the MakeCode website, the main micro:bit website at https://microbit.org/code/ gives you resources in many different coding languages for making micro:bit gadgets! Exploring with these files is a good way to get started with a new language, such as Python.

MakeCode doesn't use a login system, so the files you create live in your browser on your computer. You can't access the files from other browsers or computers.

TIP

LOOKING AT DAILY HUMAN CHALLENGES

As you go through your day, try to notice some of the little things that could be done better — and then think about how you could use your coding skills to fix them. Can you build a Scratch game to quiz you on your Spanish vocabulary? Can you build a micro:bit alarm gadget that messages you when someone moves your backpack? You might be able to turn some of your ideas into apps that could help people save time or money — or improve the safety and happiness of their lives!

ENTERING SOME CONTESTS

One way to spark ideas is to enter coding competitions. The annual Congressional App Challenge (www.congressionalappchallenge.us) invites students to code an app that will be useful to people in their community. One student team came up with an app to help local veterans find nearby support resources. Another contest, the Games for Change Student Challenge (www.gamesforchange.org/studentchallenge), invites students to make computer games that "make a difference" on themes such as Endangered Species, Disrupting Aging, or Automated Communities 2050. New contest sponsors and events appear online all the time — just Google *student app development contests* to see what's out there!

GETTING YOUR SCRATCH PROGRAMS INTO THE WORLD

A great way to dive deep in the world of coding is to share your work, showing it to the public. Doing so lets other people use your apps and give feedback on your work. Here's how to share your work in Scratch.

SHARING A PROJECT IN SCRATCH

Scratch provides a great set of tools for sharing your work with the world. After you have completed a project, follow these steps to share it:

1 At the top of the workspace, click or press the See Project Page button.

2 At the project page, click or press the orange Share button.

3 In the empty Instructions box, type information about how to use your program. In the Notes and Credits box, type any additional information you want to provide.

These notes tell people how to start and use your program. The image at the beginning of the chapter shows a project page of one of my programs, Pizza Parlor.

4 If you want to add your project to a Scratch studio, click or press the Add to Studio button (bottom right).

5 To copy the link to your shared project, click or press the Copy Link button (bottom right).

You can give people this link by email or by using any social media platform you want.

STARTING YOUR OWN SCRATCH STUDIO

You can start your own Scratch studio, like the studios you saw earlier in "Getting inspiration from Scratchers"! This is a great way to organize your work when you have a lot of programs you want to share. When you create a studio, you are its *manager*, so you can add your projects and other people's shared projects to the studio. You can choose to let people leave comments about the projects — or not. For details on starting and operating a Scratch studio, see my *Coding for Kids for Dummies*, 2nd Edition (Wiley) book or Google *how to start a Scratch studio*.

TECHNICAL STUFF

You can share your work in MakeCode, but it's not one of MakeCode's stronger features.

MAKING YOUR GADGETS REAL

Adding hardware to your MakeCode program brings your code to life! You can create your code in MakeCode, test it in the simulator, and then make a gadget real for less than $20. All you need is a micro:bit board, cable, and battery pack — the kit is available on Amazon.

PUTTING A PROGRAM ON THE MICRO:BIT BOARD

You can transfer and run a MakeCode program on the micro:bit board by following these steps:

1 **Connect the micro:bit board to the micro USB end of the cable and connect your computer to the USB end of the cable.**

When connected, an icon for the micro:bit board appears on your desktop.

2 **At the MakeCode dashboard, at the bottom of the screen, type a name for your program and then click the Save button.**

You may have already done this when you created your code.

3 **In MakeCode, click the purple Download button at the bottom of the screen.**

A .hex file downloads to your computer (usually to your Downloads folder).

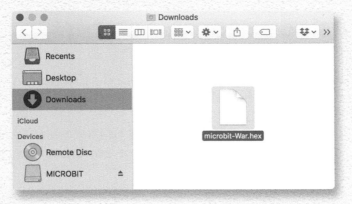

4 **Drag the .hex file from your computer to the icon for the micro:bit device (shown in the Devices area on your desktop).**

Your code is copied to the micro:bit. During the transfer, the orange micro:bit indicator button (on the back of the board) blinks quickly. When the blinking stops, the transfer is complete.

5 **Power the board.**

The micro:bit needs power to operate. Power the board by leaving it connected to your computer via the USB cable. Or to make the device portable, attach the battery pack to the micro:bit (and disconnect it from your computer).

Your micro:bit should now run the program you coded and transferred onto the board.

REMEMBER

The micro:bit stores in its memory only the last program transferred to it. If you change your program in MakeCode, you must drag the updated program onto the micro:bit.

ADDING MORE HARDWARE

Memory, sensors, and many other *components* (electronic pieces) are packed on one little micro:bit board. But you can still add new components to your micro:bit to make your gadget do even more things! Here are a few cool examples:

» **External sounds:** Add alligator clip wires and a cheap speaker to make sounds play out loud.

» **Snazzier electronic games and toys:** Buy a few extras such as bendy wires, modeling clay (nonconductive), and duct tape. With these you can make a frustration toy, Bop It games, and rock, paper, scissors bracelets. (Search online to find out how!)

» **Professional packaging:** Design and 3D-print accessories to attach to your micro:bit, such as a Magic 8-ball shell! Check out the free TinkerCad 3D-design interface at www.tinkercad.com to see how you can make your own objects and view libraries of creations by other kids.

» **Bigger and bolder components:** Go all out and buy (from www.dfrobot.com) a Boson Kit, which includes an expansion board for your micro:bit and modular components such as a sound sensor, and a servo motor.

Learn more about the layout of the micro:bit board, including how to use its sensors, in the micro:bit Features section of the MakeCode website at https://microbit.org/guide/features/. Or check out the micro:bit sensor information and extra projects I provide in Coding for Kids for Dummies, 2nd Edition (Wiley)!

TECHNICAL

UPPING YOUR GAME

You can grow your new coding skills in lots of different ways. Here are some ways you can kick it up a notch.

AT-HOME LEARNING

You can continue learning to code at home, through online courses and subscriptions at low or no cost. Many online courses at all levels are available, with each course teaching you new concepts through video, code examples, and code runners. *Code runners* are places that let you build and run code, and then check the code to make sure it works. Many online courses are free, such as those from Code.org (https://code.org), CodeHS (https://codehs.com), and Khan Academy (www.khanacademy.org). Some of the for-pay options might be worth it at both introductory and higher levels. For example Code Monkey (www.playcodemonkey.com) and BitsBox (https://bitsbox.com) offer uniquely fun, kid-friendly, guided projects. And CoderZ (https://gocoderz.com) provides top-notch lessons in coding for virtual robotics. Perform a Google search of *online coding courses and classes for kids* to find the latest offerings.

CAMPS AND CLUBS

After-school camps, school-break camps, and summer camps are all great ways to rev up your coding skills and meet other kids who are interested in coding. Name brand camps such as iDTech (www.idtech.com) and Digital Media Academy (www.digitalmediaacademy.org) provide excellent experiences — but expect to pay several hundred dollars or more to attend.

One of the coolest camps for tweens and teens is hosted by NuVu (https://cambridge.nuvustudio.com). There, you can design and code in themed sessions such as Cyborg Enhancements and Digital Street Fashion. Universities in your area might also host low- or no-cost camps on coding and STEM themes. Check the websites of universities near you to find out the availability of these programs.

You might also be able to find a coding club at your school or in your community. National organizations such as Girls Who Code (https://girlswhocode.com), Black Girls Code (www.blackgirlscode.com), and other groups provide volunteers and field trips to help you continue your coding journey and connect with like-minded kids. Do a Google search of *coding camps and clubs* to find out what's available in your area.

BOOKS

Dummies books — like the one you're reading now! — are fabulous, inexpensive guides for learning how to code in new languages. Each of the following books features a different language and provides several fun and instructional coding projects in that language, perfect for kids and tweens:

» *Coding For Kids For Dummies,* 2nd Edition, by Camille McCue, PhD

» *JavaScript For Kids For Dummies* by Chris Minnick and Eva Holland

- » *Minecraft Modding For Kids For Dummies* by Sarah Guthals, PhD, Stephen Foster, PhD, and Lindsey Handley, PhD

- » *Python For Kids For Dummies* by Brendan Scott

- » *Raspberry Pi For Kids For Dummies* by Richard Wentk

- » *Ruby For Kids For Dummies* by Christopher Haupt

- » *Scratch For Kids For Dummies* by Derek Breen

There are many other books on specialty coding topics that you might enjoy. One of my favorites, *Sew Electric* by Leah Buechley and Kanjun Qui (HLT Press), shows you how to make and code wearable and soft electronics using a Tiny Lily (Arduino electronics board) and the C programming language.

SOUPING UP USER INTERFACES IN SCRATCH

You may have noticed already that building great apps and gadgets takes more than knowing how to code. Although designing your user interface (UI) isn't coding, it is an important part of creating technologies that people enjoy and understand how to use. This section offers a bit of guidance to help you get fancier with your design work. For adding custom images, Scratch lets you paint your own images or upload images you find online. And for adding custom sounds, Scratch lets you record your own sounds or upload sounds you find online.

PAINTING YOUR OWN IMAGES

To paint your own sprite for a project, click and hold down on the Add a Sprite button and then choose the Paint option. A new sprite is created, and the Scratch costume editor opens for you to paint your sprite. To add your own backdrop to your project, click and hold down on the Add a Backdrop button and then choose the Paint option. A new backdrop is created, and the Scratch backdrop editor opens for you to paint your backdrop.

When painting your own creations in the Scratch image editors, you have lots of tools and colors to choose from. You can work in bitmap mode or vector mode. *Bitmap mode* lets you paint at the pixel level, which means after you've added colors and shapes to the canvas, you can't edit them individually. *Vector mode* lets you keep the properties of each individual shape you add to the canvas, so you can edit the size, shape, and color of each part of your image at any time.

FINDING IMAGES ONLINE

Using Google image search, you can search for new images to use in your projects. Type any search term that describes the image you want. Click Images to see all the images. Click the Tools button and choose Usage ⇨ Labeled for Reuse to narrow the images to only those you can use legally.

You can narrow the image search also by size. Large images are good for backgrounds, and small or thumbnail images are good for objects that go in front of the background, such as costumes on sprites. Also, by searching for only .png images, you can find images that have transparent backgrounds. This type of image can go in front of the background.

On a computer, save an image you want by Ctrl-clicking (Mac) or right-clicking (Windows) the image. On a tablet, click the Options button that appears with the image. When the pop-up menu appears, choose Save Image As and name the image. Use a short name that makes sense to you. Then, to use the image as a custom sprite in your project, click and hold down on the Add a Sprite button and choose the Upload option. Find and select the image you saved on your computer. Or to add a custom backdrop to your project, click and hold down on the Add a Backdrop button and choose the Upload option. Find and select the image you saved.

RECORDING YOUR OWN SOUNDS

You can create your own sounds to use in your Scratch projects! You can also produce vocals, sound effects, and noises from any location (think city streets or a public pool). To record a sound in Scratch, switch to the Sounds tab and then hover your cursor over the Choose a Sound icon in the bottom-left corner and choose Record from the menu that appears. The recording is added to your sound assets for the current project. To make adjustments to a sound, use the editing tools in the Scratch sound editor.

FINDING SOUNDS ONLINE

The web offers millions of sounds you can use in your Scratch projects. For a giant collection of free sound effects in .mp3 and .wav formats, go to www.SoundBible.com. Another cool source of sounds is the Video Game Music Archive (www.vgmusic.com), which has almost every video game sound, including those from really old platforms. (I found the opening music of Dig Dug for the Atari 2600!) Most of the sounds on this site are in .midi format.

Scratch accepts sound files in .mp3 and .wav formats. If you create or find a sound file in a different format (such as .midi), you'll need to download it, save it, and convert it before using it in these programming environments. Programs such as GarageBand let you open .midi files and convert them to the .mp3 format.

On most sound sites, save a sound you want by Ctrl-clicking (Mac) or right-clicking (Windows) the sound. On a tablet, click the Options button that appears with the sound. When the pop-up menu appears, choose Save Sound As and name the sound. Use a short name that makes sense to you. (Check that you have permission to download the sound and use it royalty-free.) To upload a saved sound in Scratch, switch to the Sounds tab. Click and hold down on the Choose a Sound icon in the bottom left of the Scratch dashboard, and then choose Upload Sound From the pop-up menu that appears.

NEXT STEPS

Fast-forward 5, 10, and 15 years down the road. How far do you want to take your coding skills? Here's a glimpse of your possible future.

CODING AT SCHOOL

Take as many computer science courses as your school offers. In high school, you may be able to take AP Computer Science Principles (AP CSP) and AP Computer Science A (which teaches Java); you can even earn college credit if you do well in these courses. Also sign up for courses in robotics, engineering, design of all types, advanced math, and advanced science. And don't forget — any course that teaches you to communicate well in speech, writing, and images is going to help you, too!

CODING IN COLLEGE

More and more universities are offering degree programs in coding and related fields in computer science. Some of the most prestigious programs are offered at big-name universities, but others are at tech-focused schools such as Full Sail (www.fullsail.com), which boasts grads who work on productions including Marvel movies, and Make School (www.makeschool.com), which doesn't charge you anything until after you've graduated and started working!

Each school has a different focus, such as programming, human-computer interaction, robotics, data analytics, artificial intelligence, and virtual reality. Every school has its own entry requirements and acceptance rates. Start learning about your options now so that you can get on a path that leads you to your destination.

Additionally, start creating a portfolio of websites and apps — and control code for electronic and robotic devices — so that you can showcase your work and rise to the top of the pile of students applying for admission.

CODING AS A CAREER

Careers that require a knowledge of coding are on the rise. Having a career in coding means many different things, and many options are available to you. You might choose an entrepreneurial path, building apps you sell in the App Store and the Google Play Store. You might choose to make websites for companies. You might work in marketing or government as a social media guru. Or maybe you'll be part of a team looking at data for sales or sports or medicine or politics. You could work in the arts, coding virtual museums, 4D roller coaster rides, or interactive playgrounds — like teamLab's Connecting Block Town, which digitally connects physical objects in real-time to create a colorful map (www.teamlab.art).

You could get involved in architecture and city planning, designing and coding smart cities and homes of the future. Perhaps you'll work in personal electronics, creating cool new wearables for fashion, fitness, or health tracking. Or perhaps you want to work at a university or corporate research facility, inventing new languages and applications.

Whatever path you choose, you've made a smart choice in learning to code. And whether you pursue a coding career or not, your new coding skills will boost your education and career options in the year to come. Congratulations, you've reached the end — and it's only the beginning!

DEDICATION

I dedicate this book to my extraordinary parents — my Mom, Beverly Dempsey-Moody, and my Dad, the late Eric Moody, PhD — for their role modeling of what it means to work tirelessly and investigate the wonders of the world through the lens of STEM.

ABOUT THE AUTHOR

Camille McCue, PhD, is an educator and author who loves helping people everywhere grow their skills and confidence in the STEM/ CS fields. She teaches everyone from kindergarteners to graduate students, and everything from computer science and math to Future Cities Engineering and Physics. Working for organizations from NASA and PBS to the Adelson Educational Campus and Project Lead the Way, Camille is a longtime Dummies author who has now written 11 books for Wiley. She earned her BA in mathematics (University of Texas at Austin) and her doctorate in curriculum and instruction (UNLV). Camille and her awesome family (Michael, Ian, Carson, and a pack of fur babies) live in Las Vegas — and a little bit in New York City.

AUTHOR'S ACKNOWLEDGMENTS

I'd like to acknowledge the always excellent team at Wiley, especially my longtime executive editor, Steve Hayes, for publishing this second edition of *Getting Started with Coding*. I would also like to thank my outstanding project editor, Susan Pink, who — in the Game of Thrones tradition — deserves a few extra titles, including Prognosticator-of-Page-Count, Eliminator-of-Redundancy, and Queen-of-the-Timeline.

PUBLISHER'S ACKNOWLEDGMENTS

Executive Editor: Steve Hayes

Project Editor: Susan Pink

Copy Editor: Susan Pink

Sr. Editorial Assistant: Cherie Case

Production Editor: Siddique Shaik